Crystal Night

Crystal Night

9–10 NOVEMBER 1938

RITA THALMANN and
EMMANUEL FEINERMANN

Translated by Gilles Cremonesi

**HOLOCAUST LIBRARY
NEW YORK**

Translated from the French *La Nuit de Cristal: 9-10 November 1938*
Copyright © 1972 by Editions Robert Laffont, S.A., Paris
English translation copyright © 1974 by Thames and Hudson, Ltd., London

Publication of this book was made possible
by a grant from Benjamin and Stefa Wald

Cover design by Eric Gluckman
Printed in the United States of America
by Waldon Press, Inc., New York City.

Library of Congress Catalog Card Number: 73-78757

Contents

Illustrations follow page 96

Introduction

The pogrom of November 1938 had all the features of a classical tragedy, even a poetic name, 'Crystal Night', given it later by the Nazis because of the tons of shattered glass that strewed the German cities after it had taken place. Greater Germany (Germany, Austria and the Sudeten territories) provided the unity of place; there was unity of time – the action occurred on the night of November 9th; and there was unity of action in the terrorization and indiscriminate persecution of the Jews, designed to force them to leave their country and their possessions.

It was a tragedy in five acts whose chronology is a schematic résumé of the Jews' fate under the National Socialist government.

After 1933, when the Nazis took power, terror against the Jews in Germany progressively escalated. Unlike other groups persecuted by the regime, the Jews could not withdraw into silence or hiding, because no matter how they behaved, their 'racial identity' condemned them to public vengeance. First their shops were boycotted and their jobs and civil rights were removed. Then they were made to declare the value of their possessions. They were bullied by the civil service and the police and often arrested and forced to sell their property for a pittance. The climax was reached with the assassination of the Third Secretary at the German embassy in Paris by a seventeen-year-old Jew, Herschel Grynszpan, who wanted to avenge his parents' expulsion, together with fifteen thousand other Polish

Jews, from Germany to the limbo of Zbonszyn. This assassination furnished the Nazis with the ideal pretext for a manhunt.

The night of November 9th–10th 1938, the 'Crystal Night', was organized by the Nazi chiefs and their thugs with technical skill and precision. It marked the beginning of the plan, to rob the Jews of their possessions for the benefit of the Reich, and then to sweep them for ever from the German scene. At this date the 'final solution' had not yet been suggested, but Goering's and Goebbels' pronouncements left no doubt as to what the fate of the German Jews would be if other countries refused them entry or if war broke out.

The outside world was apprised of events in Germany, particularly the Great Powers – Soviet Russia, the United States, Great Britain and France – but merely protested more or less vigorously without lifting a finger to organize the massive rescue which would be needed while there was still time.

Then the war broke out. Its toll in lives and suffering was the consequences of the weakness – not say cowardice – which permitted Hitler to reinforce his power and to endow Germany's arsenals with unprecedented strength. When the regime finally fell, the conquerors learned with astonishment the magnitude of the Nazi crimes. The Nazi leaders were brought before a tribunal at Nuremberg. But no one judged the other crime, of which the larger part of the so-called civilized world was guilty through failing to help people in danger. The significant episode of the 'Crystal Night', which we propose to deal with in this volume, illuminates this other crime.

Our account is based entirely on properly authenticated documents and testimony. Compiling it has not been a pleasant task. We have been concerned exclusively with the accuracy and authenticity of facts and not, as is too often the case in books of this kind, with sensational or morbid detail.

We should like to thank the National Archive in Washington, the Yad Washem Institute in Jerusalem, the Centre de Documentation Juive Contemporaine, the Bibliothèque de Documentation Internationale Contemporaine and the Bibliothèque National of Paris, the Central Archive of the German Democratic Republic in Potsdam, the many regional and local archives in the German Federal Republic and, last but not least, the friendly and helpful staff of the Wiener Library in London. All have assisted us with great understanding in our long and sometimes difficult task of research.

We are aware that many gaps have yet to be filled in order to complete our knowledge of this hitherto neglected episode in the history of the Third Reich. Such as it is, our work aims to rise above the anecdotal level to which studies of the recent past are too often confined. Apart from the tragedy of November 1938 itself, we wish to emphasize that the isolated crucible of the 'Crystal Night' became a conflagration that engulfed half the world because there was no one to contain it.

Nearer to us now there are other crucibles, such as the Middle East ...

Paris, November 1971

RITA THALMANN
EMMANUEL FEINERMANN

1

1938, the Decisive Year

The year 1938 was looked on as decisive not only by post-war historians, but at the time by the German Foreign Minister, Ribbentrop, who stated as much in a circular entitled 'The Jewish Question, a Factor in our Foreign Policy for 1938' which he issued to diplomatic and consular offices on January 25th 1939.[1] 'It is not by chance,' the document stated, 'that 1938, the year of our destiny, saw the realization of our plan for Greater Germany as well as a major step towards the solution of the Jewish problem.'

The text was framed in the pompous, coldly authoritarian style of official Nazi communications. 'The spread of Jewish influence,' it went on, 'and its corruption of our political, economic and cultural life has perhaps done more to undermine the German people's will to prevail than all the hostility shown us by the Allied powers since the Great War. This disease in the body of our people had first to be eradicated before the Great German Reich could assemble its forces in 1938 to overcome the will of the world.'

The decisive year, as the German Foreign Minister called it, opened with the concentration of political power in Hitler's hands in February. Opposition within Germany had been rooted out, compulsory military service had been revived and Germany had claimed a place in international politics. The Nazis now felt strong enough to cast off the last representatives of the old government who had supported their rise to power. Both General Blomberg, the Minister of

War, and General von Fritsch, the Commander-in-Chief of the Wehr-macht, were dismissed; the army did not dare protest. The servile Walter Funk, who had first secured industrial backing for Hitler in 1930, took over responsibility for the economy from Dr Schacht. Old Baron von Neurath was replaced by the erratic and idiosyncratic Ribbentrop in the Ministry of Foreign Affairs. Hitler felt that the time was now ripe to implement his 'grand design'. He had first defined this to his colleagues at a meeting on November 5th 1937: 'Taking risks to ensure the security and expansion of the racial community'—in other words, German supremacy by force and, if necessary, by war.[2]

The Jews were not forgotten in this 'grand design'. Since coming to power, the leaders of the Third Reich had continually broadcast their hatred of the Jews and their plan to rid Germany of them for ever. In April 1933 violent antisemitic demonstrations had opened a campaign to boycott Jewish shops. A succession of laws had excluded Jews from public office and from certain professions (journalism, publishing, radio, the cinema) where they 'perverted the national spirit'. In consequence 37,000 Jews fled the country.[3] After 1934, however, the death of President Hindenburg, the open revolt of the SA and the mounting restlessness of the military chiefs forced the Nazi leaders to concentrate on reinforcing their positions. The wave of persecutions slackened. In fact the Nazi authorities were particu-larly eager to assuage Jewish businessmen's fears because their services were vital to the Germany economy.

In a statement of January 17th 1934 the Minister of the Interior emphasized that the legislation disqualifying Jews from public office and certain professions 'did not extend to the private sector'. And another issued by the Minister of Labour in November 1934 an-nounced that 'Jewish employees have the same rights as Aryans'. A special service was set up to hear complaints by Jews who had suffered discrimination.

These measures encouraged most of the Jews remaining in the Reich to hope that they would find a way of living with their new masters. 'We cannot,' stated the newspaper of the Central Verein, the principal association of Jews in Germany, on February 4th 1934, 'abandon the ideals of German civilization and spirit. . . . We recognize the need which the German nation feels to determine with our help and that of the other Jewish organizations in Germany the extent and the limits of our activities and the nature and forms of our co-operation.' The President of the Jewish German Veterans Association echoed in the *Schild* of April 12th 1934 : 'Our country can solve the Jewish problem provided that racial discrimination does not lead to racial defamation which would, in our estimation, be unacceptable and unjust in view of our past record.'

The same theme dominated the national conferences of the Hilfsverein (Society for Jewish Aid) in May 1934 and June 1935. Even the racial laws of Nuremberg, publicized in September 1935 so as to hasten Jewish emigration, did not cause an increase in departures. Between 1934 and 1937 Jews emigrated at a steady rate of 20,000 – 25,000 a year, of which number 22.1 per cent. were under twenty; 45.6 per cent. were between twenty and forty; 15.6 per cent. were between forty and fifty; 16.7 per cent. were over fifty.

Those who emigrated did so because they were in danger, either on account of their past political involvements or because they had lost their jobs under the racial laws. A few well-to-do families had wanted to secure the safety of their fortunes outside Germany. Most of the emigrants were reluctant to accept a radical change of scene. Half of them remained in western Europe, and a third of these in France. Twenty-seven per cent. went to Palestine, where they made up no more than 22 per cent. of the immigrants who arrived during these years. The United States immigration statistics are still more surprising. Although the annual quotas permitted 130,000 German-born Jews to settle in the United States between 1933 and 1937, it is estimated that only 27,000 actually did so.

After five years of National Socialism, the German government angrily acknowledged that threats and intimidation had not rid the Reich of its Jews. About a quarter of the total had fled but the other three-quarters still preferred to stay in Germany. The government concluded that it would have to change tactics in order to obtain better results.

By a coincidence, though certainly not by chance, the first warning anticipated Hitler's formal announcement of his policy. It appeared on October 14th 1937 in an article in *Das Schwarze Korps,* the SS magazine which seemed to play the role of herald at every stage in the evolution of policies towards the Jews. The article discussed the inconsistency between the social status and the economic status of Jews in the Reich. Although excluded from political and cultural activities, and from intermarriage with non-Jews, in Germany, they still wielded power in industry and commerce. This anomaly had to be corrected, the SS magazine urged: 'Today we no longer need Jewish business.'

After this, the government and the Party increasingly urged the sale of Jewish shops and businesses to Aryans. After February 1938, when all powers were concentrated in the hands of the Führer, the clamour became markedly more strident.

The start of a new phase was announced by Julius Streicher, the sinister District Leader of the Nazi Party in Nuremberg and editor of the *Stürmer,* a magazine which specialized in pornographic anti-semitism. Streicher, who had been a leader in the persecutions of 1933, told a group of foreign journalists that in the event of a war the Germans would destroy the Jews. The same theme was taken up again in March 1938 in an article signed by Alfred Rosenberg, one of the ideological spokesmen of the Party. It became a leitmotif of the Nazi leaders.

After this, events succeeded one another rapidly and it is difficult to establish their chronology. Three separate events, however, of apparently contrasting significance, which occurred during the years 1937-38, marked a definite change in Hitler's policy towards the Jews.

First, in 1937 the USSR had deported a number of Germans, whereupon the Reich decided to deport five hundred Russian Jews resident in Germany. Germany and Soviet Russia at this time had no common frontier. When the USSR refused to receive the five hundred Jews the Nazis confined them in a concentration camp, without arousing any protest from a single foreign government.

Second, whereas the Nazi government had always attacked the

Jews as non-Aryans, in 1938 it began actively to attack Jewish institutions for the first time. A new decree withdrew the status of 'corporations by public law', which had previously protected Jewish institutions just as it protected Christian institutions. Again, this measure aroused no protests.

Third, in the few weeks which followed the annexation of Austria on March 13th 1938, the 192,000 Austrian Jews, of which ninety-five per cent. lived in Vienna, then the third largest centre of Jewry in Europe, suffered greater persecutions than the German Jews had suffered during the previous five years.

In March 1938 the leaders of the Reich had two worries concerning the Jews. On the one hand there were at least 600,000 Jews in Germany, excluding Christians of Jewish descent and children of mixed marriages, while, on the other, the personal greed of the Austrian Nazis (who were freely seizing Jewish goods and property) threatened to take hold in Germany and disrupt German rearmament, which required every form of economic support available. Goering, the master-mind of the Four Year Plan, accordingly announced in Vienna on March 26th 1938 that policy concerning the disposal of Jewish possessions, not only in Austria but throughout the whole of the Reich, would have to be regulated by legislation.

Methods were often made legal after the fact. Antisemitic measures were first tested on a local basis. A higher authority would then rule whether it was in the 'best interests of the state' to drop them or adopt them throughout the Reich. In the meantime a decree of April 26th obliged Jews to declare the value of their goods and property to the authorities under penalty of criminal prosecution. Article 7 of the decree authorized the Director of the Four Year Plan (Goering) to dispose of the property declared 'according to the needs of the German economy.'[4] A few days later Rudolf Brinkmann, the Under Secretary of State in charge of the economy, explained at a press conference that this decree was intended to accelerate Jewish emigration.[5]

Other forms of intimidation soon followed. The antisemitic campaign launched in Austria after the Anschluss in March inspired a fresh campaign to boycott Jewish shops in many German cities. A

regulation requiring Jews to write their names in large white charac-
ters on their shop windows made boycotting easier and was to play a
significant role in the November pogroms.

Then, in mid-June some fifteen hundred Jews were rounded up
and detained in concentration camps; 146 of them died at Buchenwald alone during the next three months. Most of them had previously
been convicted with suspended sentences on trivial charges such as
infringements of traffic laws, or of housing or labour regulations.
These previous convictions permitted them to be classed as 'undesirables arrested on suspicion'.

In Berlin huge round-ups were carried out in the cafés and on the
main routes under the direction of General Daluege, the Chief of
Police, as well as at Stoelpchensee, the last open-air swimming pool
in the Berlin suburbs to admit Jews. Daluege's brother-in-law, who
was Police Inspector at Berlin-Charlottenburg, displayed remarkable
ingenuity in keeping the Jewish population in a constant state of
anxiety. He would arrest individuals and keep them in custody for
two or three hours on the grounds that their passports had expired or
their identification papers were incomplete, and would then release
them after entering their names in his records. He also developed a
new method of harassing and trapping Jews. He would have pedes-
trians arrested for jay-walking on the main streets. If they were Aryan
they were released on payment of the usual fine of one mark. If they
were Jewish they were taken to a police station where they were
detained for at least a day and then fined between 50 and 500 marks.
Thereafter the records showed that they had been convicted on suspended sentences and could be treated as 'undesirables arrested on
suspicion'. The police also concentrated on Jews' cars, which were
assigned licence plate numbers above 350,000 for easy identification.
Most Jewish car-owners preferred to give up driving. The Machia-
vellian police inspector's methods proved particularly effective near
the main gates of Jewish cemeteries and hospitals, where passers-by
were frequently preoccupied by worry or grief and failed to notice the
near-by policemen.

Police stations began calling on rabbis or leaders of Jewish communities to help draw up lists of the Jews living in each part of various cities. In Munich the Jews were dealt a more painful surprise.[6] The Nazi authorities deliberately chose June 8th, the day when the congress of German rabbis was meeting in Munich, to inform the president of the principal synagogue in the city that he must evacuate it within twenty-four hours.

Emmanuel Kirschner, Reader of the Munich Congregation and a singing instructor at the Royal Bavarian Music Academy, returned home from an outing on the afternoon of June 8th to find his cantor waiting for him with Rabbis Bauerwald and Oels, his guests during the congress. The three men told him what had happened and asked him if he would conduct the farewell service that evening. Kirschner had celebrated the inauguration of the synagogue fifty-one years before.

The last service was attended by the whole community. When the scrolls and their appointments were removed from the Ark for safe-keeping, women and children rushed forward weeping to kiss them for the last time. At dawn the following morning the pneumatic drills began work while dynamite was used to demolish the sturdier sections of the building. A fortnight later a parking lot replaced the synagogue, which had been expropriated for a tenth of its value.

After Munich, where the National Socialist Party headquarters was located, it was the turn of Nuremberg, the site of annual Party conferences. The annals of Nuremberg,[7] where the Jews had first been welcomed at the beginning of the thirteenth century, offered the city's modern thugs a rich and elaborate tradition of persecution.

In 1348 King Charles authorized the razing of the Jewish quarters to provide space for a market. The principal synagogue of the time was replaced by a church. In the ensuing pogrom 570 men, women and children perished. Survivors were deprived of their property and expelled. Four years later they were asked back to lift the city out of the economic slump which had set in, on condition that they made no attempt to recover moneys previously owed them. A century later the citizens again petitioned for the expulsion of the Jews, this time, to Emperor Maximilian. Again, most of the deportees remained in the surrounding district until the storm blew over, but the better-educated Jews preferred not to return and settled in Prague or Salonica (where, as evidence of their origins, a book of prayers from the Nuremberg ritual was published). During this second pogrom Jewish shops were sacked and the Jews' possessions were confiscated with the support, and often to the material benefit, of the town notables. The celebrated sculptor Veit Stoss appears among the 'acquirers of Jewish goods', while Willibald Pirkheimer, who figures in German textbooks for his wisdom and charm and his edifying career as a humanist, acted as representative of the city in disposing of the immovable property which had been confiscated. Even the Jewish cemetery was pillaged. The tombstones were re-used in a number of buildings, notably in the steps leading up to the Churches of St Sebaldus and St Lawrence, where traces of Hebrew inscriptions are still visible.

In the centuries following Nuremberg unfortunately became a bastion of antisemitism. No Jew was allowed to live in Nuremberg until 1839, when a residence permit was granted to a Jewish post-coach driver who had served six years in the light cavalry of Count Thurn und Taxis and twelve years in the Munich police. A Jewish congregation was not founded for another twenty years and permission to build a synagogue was not granted for ten years more. A number of local newspapers published articles on the inauguration of the synagogue in 1872. One of them went so far as to suggest that it was a sort of expiation for the horrors previously visited on the Jews. At the ceremony to open the building the mayor declared that he was all the more pleased to be doing so because his ancestor Ulrich Stromer had driven the Jews out of the city by fire and sword in 1349. He concluded prophetically, 'With nations as with individuals, the manner of dealing with the Jewish question has always been a touchstone of civilization and humanity.'

Between 1873 and 1920 the Jewish population in Nuremberg increased by ten thousand. Some of the new arrivals had fled from pogroms in the East. In Nuremberg they seemed to find peace and stability. In 1920, however, the malignant Julius Streicher, an obscure Franconian teacher who carried a truncheon and wore boots, arrived on the scene surrounded by a band of antisemitic thugs. They terrorized the region. In the thirteen years preceding the Nazi seizure of power two hundred cases of profanation of cemeteries were recorded, mostly in small villages near Nuremberg. Long before the rise of Nazism the Franconian Jews had been frightened out of participating in the public life of the region. In 1923 the myth of Jewish ritual murders at Easter was revived, and Streicher's antisemitic campaign reached a new pitch. The Jewish community had to set up a night watch to ward off possible attacks.

After 1933 Streicher's territory became 'hell on earth' for the Jews. Three months after the boycott of Jewish shops began in April 1933, three hundred prominent Jews were arrested. Most were members of the B'nai Brith lodge. They were beaten and dragged through Nuremberg before a jeering crowd to a sports field of the SA. Here they were forced to undergo unpleasant ordeals such as clearing grass from the ground with their teeth. The heads of Aryan women who had befriended Jews were shaven and they were made to carry placards while the public jeered. During the Party conference of 1934 a Gestapo agent was forced to request police assistance in a synagogue where three to four thousand uniformed SA were about to disrupt the Jewish New Year services.

It was in this climate of hatred and violence, far more brutal than anywhere else in Germany, that an official order to expropriate the main synagogue and the administrative buildings attached to it was issued to the Jewish congregation in Nuremberg on June 18th 1938. After long deliberations the leaders of the Nuremberg synagogue, unlike their counterparts in Munich, decided unanimously never to consent to the demolition. When they refused to yield to pressure the town council, at a meeting on August 3rd 1938, voted to dispossess the congregation under a law of October 4th 1937, which authorized the renovation of German cities, and under the Führer's decree of April 9th 1938 regarding buildings in the city in which Party conferences were held.

At this meeting the Burgermeister, Liebel, made a long speech[8] in which he reminded the counsellors of their historic mission to correct the errors of their predecessors. 'Mesmerized by Jewish ideas about democracy,' he said, his predecessors, sitting in this very room, had granted permission for the Jews to construct 'that insolently oriental-looking' building in the heart of the most ancient and revered section of the city. After a few ironic comments on the 'servants of Yaweh,' who could hold their services in future in their other synagogue, which only held five hundred people, the Burgermeister apologized for any inconvenience which the demolition might cause. It was a small burden to bear, he added, considering that they would hence-forth be spared the spectacle of Jews conducting their sordid affairs on their way to and from their synagogue.

The Jews were alerted by the press and had just enough time during the night to remove the scrolls of the Law. The famous Jews' Stone which dated from 1349 was also rescued. The secretary of the congregation was later called to the Gestapo and accused of attempt-ing to smuggle it to America. (It weighed over six hundred pounds.)

The demolition of the synagogue had to be completed before the Party conference opened in September. Streicher immediately or-ganized a spectacular ceremony to which he invited local Nazi dignitaries and representatives of the German press. At 10.15 on the morning of August 10th 1938 Streicher appeared on a podium over-looking a large crowd personally to manoeuvre the crane which was to dismantle the great Star of David that surmounted the cupola. Then his henchmen dynamited the walls and the supporting pillars. The symbol of the expiation of the horrors once perpetrated against the Jews was reduced to rubble. Nuremberg slumped back into her traditional antisemitism.

A few weeks later workmen began dismantling a third synagogue, in Dortmund. The 100,000 marks granted the congregation as damages were soon recovered in fines.

The intensifying pace of the persecutions during 1938, increasingly apparent after the annexation of Austria, prompted a surge of emigra-tion applications to foreign consulates in Germany, the largest number since 1933. The American consulate was invaded by literally thousands of panic-stricken Jews. The countries bordering on the Reich refused to admit the Jews whom the Gestapo tried illegally to deport into their territories. These included Czechoslovakia, Hungary, Yugoslavia, Italy, Switzerland, Luxemburg and France. Great Britain claimed that substantial Jewish immigration into Palestine would create tension among the Arab population.

President Roosevelt was under strong pressure from public opinion but wished to avoid a great influx of refugees into the United States. He instructed Myron C. Taylor to organize an international conference which would seek some generally acceptable solution to the problem. Taylor, a former director of the American Steel Federation, declared, 'The problem of political refugees is not a matter of private interests. It is a problem requiring the intervention of governments. If we allow the flow of immigrants into states granting asylum to continue increasing chaotically, and if certain governments continue ejecting vast fractions of their populations into a world which is struggling with crisis and unprepared to accept them, then we shall be threatened with catastrophic human suffering and heightened international tension, factors which will not aid the realization of permanent peace which is the most fervent hope of all peoples.'[9]

The Evian Conference, set up by Roosevelt, reflected the conflicts of interests between the greater and lesser powers. Soviet Russia and Czechoslovakia were not represented. Italy refused the invitation, while Hungary, Rumania and Poland sent observers with the sole purpose of requesting that they, too, be relieved of their Jews. Although the leaders of the Reich refused to co-operate with the other states on the grounds that the matter concerned them alone, they allowed representatives of Jewish organizations in Germany and Austria to go to Evian. The representatives of the other thirty-two nations, which participated in the conference at the Hotel Royal between July 6th and 14th, spoke one after another, commending President Roosevelt's initiative, expressing their countries' sympathy with the victims of the persecutions and regretting that economic and social conditions within their countries precluded an increase in immigration quotas.

Lieutenant-Colonel J. W. White, the Australian Minister of Commerce and Customs, went so far as to announce that it would be unfair to others if his country granted privileges to a special category of non-British subjects. Australia had no racial problems, he added, and was not eager to import any.[10]

It was this same Lieutenant-Colonel White who was elected chairman of the sub-committee which heard the Jewish spokesmen. This proved a ludicrously fruitless exercise. In a single afternoon the sub-committee heard the representatives of forty organisations of varying importance, each with its own view of the situation. The World Jewish Congress, which represented seven million Jews, was allowed five minutes to state its case, as was the Association for Aid to German Scientists Abroad, while the delegation of Jews of the Reich was not even mentioned in the lists of groups to be heard and had to submit a written memorandum to be included in the minutes.

The *New York Herald Tribune,* in an article published on July 8th 1938, summed up the conference in a headline : 'Powers Slam Doors Against German Jews'. Dr Rosenberg, in an article of the same date published in the Nazi press under the ironic title 'What to do with Jews', stressed the evasiveness of the 'nations of emigration' and recalled their projects to establish colonies in Uganda and Madagascar.

After eight days of speeches, either elegant or poignant, the Conference closed with a resolution to continue the 'work so usefully begun at Evian'. It would reconvene under the chairmanship of George Rublee, an American diplomat, on August 3rd in London, chosen as the permanent headquarters of the International Committee.

At the request of the South American delegates, contentious allusions to the Third Reich were suppressed in the Conference's final resolution. Despite this, the German press published vehement denunciations of sympathizers with the Jews who refused to help them. JEWS FOR SALE — WHO WANTS THEM? NO ONE, announced the *Reichwart* in large type on July 14th 1938. The *Danziger Vorposten* wrote in a similar vein : 'We note that sympathy is shown the Jews so long as it encourages agitation against Germany, but no country is prepared to remove central Europe's cultural defects by accepting a few thousand Jews. The Conference has therefore vindicated the German policy towards the Jews.'

The Nazi leaders now had proof that despite indignant protests no country would actively intercede on behalf of the German and Austrian Jews. This deduction was to be sustained, during the summer and the autumn, by a number of facts.

First, when Forster, the Party District Leader of Danzig, asked Churchill in July 1938 if German legislation regarding Jews represented an obstacle to Anglo-German understanding, Churchill replied in the negative.[11]

Second, after the Anschluss the Swiss made a number of declarations and undertakings to the Nazi authorities to the effect that they would refuse Jewish refugees entry into Switzerland. In September they sent Dr Heinrich Rothmund, Chief of the Federal Police, to negotiate an agreement.[12] Under it, the Germans would not allow German Jews to cross the German–Swiss frontier without a Swiss visa or transit permit. So as to prevent this measure from applying to all German citizens, the Swiss police chief suggested that Jews' passports be specially marked. The Germans agreed. A decree of October 7th 1938 revoked German Jews' passports and replaced them with a document which bore a capital J in red ink an inch high on the left-hand side of the first page.[13]

Third, the South American countries became more restrictive, and after September 1938 most of them applied ruthless regulations to halt Jewish immigration.

Fourth, in October 1938 a French memorandum on the international Committee addressed to the German Foreign Minister stressed its purely humanitarian function. 'None of the states,' this document asserts, 'would dispute the absolute right of the German government to take with regard to certain of its citizens such measures as are within its own sovereign powers.'[14]

Hitler was perfectly right to assume that these were not merely stock phrases, since this French memorandum arrived after the Munich Agreements, under which the French and the British

23

delivered up their ally Czechoslovakia to the designs of the Reich. The powers represented on the Evian Conference seemed formally to have recognized Hitler's right to treat his nationals – for example, the Jews – as he pleased.

After the failure of the Evian Conference, a number of signs indicated that Hitler would get his own way on the Jewish question by pounding the table, a method which had so far proved effective with the Western democracies.

On August 23rd 1938 Jochen Klepper, a Protestant writer, noted in a diary (which he kept from 1933 until December 1942, when he committed suicide with his Jewish wife and his youngest daughter), 'After it was revealed at the Evian Conference that the German Jews could not expect help from abroad, everything became far more tragic.'[15]

From July to October 1938, with increasing momentum, decree after decree further limited the Jews' chances of survival in the Reich. Jewish lawyers and doctors were barred from practice and reduced to acting as legal consultants or nurses to other Jews. The professional credentials of salesmen were revoked. Shopkeepers and artisans were to be barred from any commercial activity after January 1st 1939. To the threat of unemployment was added the growing likelihood of homelessness. The Globke decree of August 17th 1938[16] required all Jewish men to change their first names to Israel and all Jewish women to Sara, besides carrying a conspicuous J in their passports. It became impossible for them to evade discrimination, particularly when hunting for lodgings. Most Aryan landlords, who either had pressure put on them by the Party or ran the hazard of exposure by informers, would not allow Jewish tenants and tried to turn out those they had as quickly as possible. The anxiety of the victims was heightened as growing numbers of Jewish landlords were forced to sell their properties.

There was no alternative to flight, while increasingly stringent exchange-control legislation, the freezing of capital under the control of the Ministries of Economics and Finance and constant rises in emigration taxes added further to the Jews' anxieties. From August

8th Jews were not allowed to open their safes except in the presence of a tax inspector. The Jews became prisoners in a country which forced them to emigrate while systematically removing their means to do so.

At a meeting of leaders of the Reich on October 14th at the Air Ministry[17] Marshal Goering, as overseer of the Four Year Plan, expounded the necessity of adapting the German economy to the growing demands of the army. In order to prepare intensively for war, which would soon break out, Marshal Goering explained that 'the Reich must eradicate doubtful elements from its population, namely the last remaining Jews. Their ejection should not be chaotic as it had been in Austria, but should benefit the Reich. "Aryanization" of Jewish property was not to be confused with charity to incompetent Nazis.' This remark provoked a sharp reply from the Austrian ministerial adviser, Fischboek, who indignantly defended his Party veterans. Goering abruptly adjourned the meeting, emphasizing that the matter would be decided by the government alone. The relevant ministries occupied themselves with implementing the sale of Jewish property, and, by November, 2,000 million of the 7,000 million marks declared as property belonging to Jews had passed into Nazi hands since April.[18]

The police were also busy. The heads of the Jewish emigration organizations were summoned with increasing frequency to Gestapo headquarters at seven in the morning and detained for hours while being urged to get on with the Jewish emigration. The SS magazine *Das Schwarze Korps,* ever the herald of new policies, could not contain its impatience for a Reich 'purified of Jews' ('judenrein').

At Buchenwald and Sachsenhausen prisoners were made to enlarge the camp, while some of the older inmates noted the arrival of fresh stocks of food and clothing. Prisoners in the Dachau workshops sewed Stars of David on thousands of striped uniforms.[19] Alarming rumours circulated amongst the Jews. Reliable sources reported a resolution at the latest Party congress that in the event of war the SS and the SA should unleash a 'Night of Long Knives' against the Jews. These rumours were substantiated by brutal pogroms in isolated towns in

Bavaria and Hesse, in which military units, mobilized at the time of the Munich crisis, had only received their demobilization orders after a delay.

Alarm quickened with the news that the Nazi authorities had deported the Sudeten Jews in mid-October, without waiting for the transfer of populations provided for in the Munich Agreements. They had been deported to Czechoslovakia, but Czechoslovakia had deported them to Hungary the next day. Hungary returned them and they were left to camp on an old barge in the Danube until some country would admit them.[20] The British minister who had asked his government to intervene on their behalf approached the Czechs, and was told that London would do better to encourage emigration and to request that the Germans cease 'dumping those unwanted Jews of occupied territories into what remains of Czechoslovakia.'[21]

Just as the accounts of this Odyssey were reaching the Jewish communities in Germany, a still more brutal event occurred.

There were in Germany and Austria some fifty thousand Jews of Polish origin. The Polish government was reluctant to allow them to return to Poland and thereby swell the ranks of the three and a half million Jews already in the country. They themselves were toying with methods which resembled the Nazis' to disperse their own Jews.[22] They now responded by introducing new regulations to prevent the repatriation of Polish Jews, and must therefore bear a heavy load of responsibility for the first large-scale deportation of the Jews from Germany which was shortly to take place.

Under a law of March 31st 1938, supplemented by an order of October 6th, Polish passports were revoked if their bearers had lived abroad for more than five years, unless a special visa were issued by the consul. The Germans, with their own experience in racial legislation, instantly realized that this Polish stratagem was aimed at the Jews. After the law took effect on October 31st the Germans would risk being left with fifteen thousand stateless Jews whom no country would admit. Berlin resolved to act quickly to avoid this danger. On October 26th the German Ambassador was ordered to inform

Warsaw that the Reich would proceed with the expulsion of Polish Jews from its territory unless the Poles formally undertook to permit them to return at any time without a special visa.[23] When, on the 27th, the Polish government expressed its refusal to agree to this condition, an order was given to the Gestapo to arrest everyone affected by the new Polish regulation and deport them surreptitiously into Poland before it took effect.[24]

As a result, fifteen thousand men, women and children were seized, herded into police stations or railway carriages with one piece of luggage each and a gratuity of 10 marks to travel the night of October 29th–30th to the German–Polish border. Trains with bolted doors and armed escorts set out from Stuttgart, Essen, Duisberg, Düsseldorf, Cologne, Hanover, Hamburg, Berlin and even Vienna. As the following report to the Gestapo from the Hanover station-master reveals, the operation was executed with Prussian precision:

'Special train SP Han. 4199 made up at 1930 – about two hours before departure. Consisting of 14 well-lit carriages each with 55 seats, of which 35–40 were occupied. The departure of the Jews, carrying large quantities of hand luggage, proceeded on platform 5, which had been closed to the public before the train was assembled. The Jews were allowed to purchase food and tobacco.

'The special train departed on schedule at 21.40, from track 11, platform 5.'[25]

'I believe that I shall not forget one instant of that day, even though I cannot remember the date,' relates Ottilie Schoenwald, founding president of the Jewish Women's Association of Bochum.[26]

It was a freezing October day. As if adhering to a Jewish tradition, the trouble began on the eve, not in the evening, but in the afternoon. The door-bell rang constantly. Our library was soon teeming with a complete cross-section of the Congregation. Amid the confusion of voices and stories I could not tell exactly what had happened.

'All Jews from the East are to be arrested.'

'No, only the Poles.'

'On the contrary, Poles are free. Stateless persons are under arrest.'

The secretary of the Congregation arrived and gave my husband, who was President of the Congregation, a more or less faithful account of what had happened. No one had been arrested yet, but Jews born in Poland were to be deported. They had to leave with their families by next morning. We didn't know whether to try to obtain a postponement, or to suggest passive resistance, or submission.

First we needed to know whether it was a local measure against which the Congregation or the Jewish organizations could protest at Party headquarters so as to obtain a postponement, or a general decision which emanated from Berlin. I telephoned the congregations at Essen and Dortmund. Despite their confirmation that it was a nation-wide decision, I rang the Berlin office of Jews of the Reich. After I had spoken with Dr Leo Baeck the facts were clear. Under these grim circumstances, it was our duty to do all we could to help the unfortunate deportees. As president of the local Association of Jewish Women, I rang the Berlin headquarters of the organization to arrange that services be made available in the main railway stations throughout Germany. Then we attacked the local problems. The few Jews who still had cars immediately set out to collect what suitcases they could find. Amid this rush every ring of the door-bell brought trouble.

'All of the men have been taken to prison.'

'Tomorrow at eight the women and children are to meet them at the station.'

'The deportees are in despair.'

'The men will not eat prison food. They want to keep Kosher.'

We didn't know what to do. As soon as the cars returned with trunks, the drivers were sent out again to buy sausages at the Jewish butchers, then to the bakers who promised to prepare hundreds of loaves of bread for the following morning. A few kind souls began cleaning a huge copper boiler to prepare a hot meal.

Early next morning we carried our provisions to the prison. We simply marched past the speechless guards straight into the court-yard where the poor Jews had been lined up just as we arrived. The guard on duty, whom I knew, advised me to distribute the food at the station. He offered to carry the steaming boiler in his own car.

A crowd of shouting and weeping women and children was already assembled at the station. In the square outside trucks un-loaded their unhappy passengers. Bochum was the assembly point for the surrounding villages, mainly populated by workers among whom there were many Jews from the east. During the First World War, when the Germans occupied Poland they had been forcibly removed to the Ruhr to replace German miners who had been conscripted. This involuntary labour force was so large that the local communities set up Jewish employment services for them. When the war was over most of them returned to their previous occupations. Those who chose to remain in Germany were re-garded as deserters and forfeited their Polish citizenship. Their children, who had come as infants or who had been born in Germany, grew up without speaking Polish.

Most of the women and children herded into the third-class waiting-rooms had been dragged out of bed without being allowed to pack. After my husband agreed that the Congregation would bear the expenses, the fleet of cars set out to search Jewish shops for covers and underclothing. The list of requests was unending, but under the circumstances displays of human weakness were merely heartbreaking.

The stationmaster informed me that the special train would not leave before eleven that evening. At our request he promised to link up a goods car so that there would be room for people to sleep in the carriages. During the ensuing lull we left in our car with a few of the deportees, undertaking to be responsible for them, to fill a few suitcases with warm clothing, especially for the children. Some could not contain their concern about business matters which they were forced to abandon. My husband, who is a lawyer, arranged for them to give power of attorney to relatives or leaders of the Congregation who would look after their interests.

Neither the food we were able to offer nor the chance to quit the icy evening air to join the women and children in the waiting-room was as comforting to these men as the powers of attorney which they granted me with precise instructions. Despite all that they had been through, these unfortunate men still believed in commercial good practice and in German justice.

An aged paralytic and a girl with a high fever both seemed unable to make the journey. Even a Nazi doctor I called could not deny this. But they both resolutely refused to be taken to hospital. They wanted to be with their families. The doctor was furious and screamed that he should not have been called out to look after a Jewish rabble.

'I took it upon myself to call you,' [Ottilie Schoenwald retorted], 'because I thought they were being deported, not sentenced to death, but I realize that these people prefer death to the prospect of remaining alone in Germany.'

The stupefied doctor handed her the order for them to be admitted to hospital. Then, pointing at her, he whispered a few words in the ear of a Gestapo officer who had witnessed the incident and who now walked off with a shrug. But the two invalids steadfastly refused to change their minds. The old man asked to be anchored to a chair so that he could be carried on to the train with his family.

As night fell, the refugees were worn out and apathetic. The last woollens had been handed out. Their hunger and thirst had been quenched. The Jews who had come to help had returned home with the kindly car owners. The babies were in their mothers' arms, while the young children slept on their mothers' laps or at their feet, making the scene incongruously peaceful. But at half-past ten the order was abruptly issued to assemble on the platform, and frenzy swept over them. Young and old ran in every direction, jostling down the platforms. Mothers called their children to lend a hand or hold on to their skirts. Children wailed. No one tried to restore order. Finally they were all on the platform with their satchels and baggage. A heap of blankets left for them on the platform aroused the envy of a band of Hitler Youth, who thought they were out on a night's jaunt. Nerves were on edge by the time the special train arrived. A long sigh, like a sob, seemed to escape from a single gigantic being. At the same moment the women and children round us closed in as if to a protective guardian. I remember telling them, 'It won't be very long before you people outside will think, "the poor people in Germany will have no one to help them when it comes to their turn to leave." You at least have someone to comfort you and shout "Mazel Tov" and "Shalom".' ['Good Luck' and 'Peace be unto you'.]

After a last handshake they roused themselves and rushed forward to find seats.

As the paralysed old man in his kaftan and his round hat, propped with dignity in his chair, was lifted on to the carriage, I heard a young Nazi remark to one of his comrades, 'Look at his face. You should make a sketch of him.'

'You just do that,' I exploded in exasperation, 'And don't you ever forget what you've seen here. May it haunt your nights until the Last Judgment.'

They smiled back with embarrassment. They assumed from the way I spoke that I could not possibly be with the others. They may have thought I was on the Nazi staff. As they were uncertain, they cautiously left without another word and without a sketch.

We all know the discomfort, the sense of desolation that we feel as trains draw out of stations, and as silence and emptiness replace the bustle and the hubbub of departure. That night I felt that desolation to the limit of endurance. I was too upset to reply to the compassionate words of the stationmaster and the Gestapo officers standing by me on the platform. They had tried to be humane while executing orders which were totally inhuman.

The punctuality, and the comparative order and courtesy, with which the journey had begun diminished as the train approached murkier illegal territory. A convoy left Berlin at 2.45 and arrived at midnight at the frontier station of Konitz, where the Polish railwaymen were amazed to find it stationary and unlit. Inside were two thousand terrified deportees. Their German escort had evaporated into the night, after threatening to shoot them if they approached windows or doors. No sleeping arrangements had been made at the station. The deportees' only refuge from the cold consisted of two waiting-rooms, where the air was so close that four of them suffocated to death. When the Jews in the surrounding area heard of their plight they brought what provisions they could. People who had owned apartments and shops in the Kurfürstendamm queued up at two in the morning for a glass of tea and a crust of bread. They resumed their journey two days later as far as Cracow, where a reception committee provided food, medicine and nurses.[27]

The ordeal of the refugees at Zbonszyn was worse. A thousand Jews from Hamburg arrived at seven in the morning after twelve hours' travel. They were made to walk the last five miles to the frontier. The Polish guards confronted them with bayonets while the German police shoved them forward with their rifle butts, shouting, 'Go on. Don't worry. They wouldn't dare shoot you.'

A few young people joined hands and ducked under the barrier, shouting at the Poles, 'Shoot.'

The guards fired into the air, at which the crowd of refugees panicked, knocked down the barriers and entered Poland. Physically and emotionally broken, they sat in the cold and rainy mud for three hours, munching their last bits of food until they were authorized to proceed to Zbonszyn. In the inns, stables and sheds of this tiny village under Polish guard they found six thousand other deportees who had already arrived. At five in the evening they were herded into the main square, where six officials sat behind tables to record their names and the names of any Polish friends or relatives likely to take them in. The crush was so great that the tables were knocked down, and the officials gave up. The next day they returned and interviewed small groups at a time, treating them as foreigners and giving them no assistance.

2

The Pretext

On November 3rd 1938, Herschel Grynszpan, a young Polish Jew living in Paris, received a post-card from his sister Berta informing him that his family had been deported from Hanover to a Polish camp at Zbonszyn.

Dear Herschel,
  You must have heard about the disaster. I shall tell you what has happened. On Thursday evening, rumours were circulating that Polish Jews in our city were being expelled. None of us believed it. At nine o'clock that evening a policeman came to our house to tell us to report to the police station with our passports. We all trooped off as we were to the police station. Practically the whole neighbourhood was already there. Almost immediately we were taken to the town hall in a police car; so was everyone else. No one told us what was up, but we realized that this was going to be the end. They shoved an expulsion order into our hands, saying we had to leave Germany before October 29th. We were not allowed to go home. I pleaded to be allowed to fetch a few things and a policeman accompanied me. I packed a case with the most important clothes, but that was all we could salvage. We haven't a penny. Could you send us something at Lodz? Love from all of us.'[1]

Berta.

This news plunged Herschel Grynszpan into deep despair. Four days later, on Monday, November 7th, at 9.35 in the morning, he approached the German Embassy in 78 Rue de Lille. Outside the Embassy Grynszpan asked François Autret, a policeman on duty, to direct him to the main entrance. The policeman pointed it out and Herschel went inside, when the concierge's wife, Mme Mathis, asked what he wanted.

'I would like to deliver an important document,' he replied.

Mme Mathis told him to present himself to Nagorka, the porter on duty on the first floor. He crossed the courtyard and climbed to the first floor, where he found Nagorka and explained that he had an important document to hand to one of the embassy secretaries. Nagorka offered to take the document, but Grynszpan declined the offer and insisted on delivering it personally. Nagorka then asked him to wait a few minutes in a waiting-room. Without asking him to fill out the customary visitor's form, the porter led him into the office of Third Secretary Ernst vom Rath, the only embassy secretary then present.

Herschel Grynszpan's father, Sendel Siegmund Grynszpan, was born at Radomsk at a time when Poland was part of Russia. His mother, Rifka Silberberg, came from the same region. In April 1911, a year after they married, the Grynszpans fled Polish Russia for fear that a tide of pogroms would sweep across the Ukrainian border into Poland.[2] They settled in Hanover, retaining Russian nationality until the end of the First World War. When the Versailles Treaty restored territorial sovereignty to Poland, Sendel Grynszpan opted for Polish nationality.

The Grynszpans had eight children. The first was stillborn on November 11th 1912. The second was born on April 27th 1914 and died of scarlet fever in 1928. A third son was killed in a road accident. A daughter, Ester Beile (Berta), was born on January 31st 1916, and another son, Marcus, on August 18th 1919. The sixth, and the last to survive, was Herschel Feibel, born March 28th 1921 in his parents' home at 36 Burgstrasse, Hanover.

The Grynszpans lived on the meagre income yielded by their tailor's shop in an old quarter of Hanover. For twenty years Sendel Grynszpan struggled to make ends meet while his family was decimated by illness and misfortune. The devastating effects of the economic slump in 1929 forced him to give up his shop until 1934. During this interval he traded in second-hand goods. His earnings were so small that he received welfare assistance. He was able to return to tailoring just as Adolf Hitler rose to power. Despite the Nazi Government, his family subsisted more or less adequately until 1938.

Then, on the night of October 28th–29th, the German Government deported the fifteen thousand Polish Jews who would have been made stateless by the law which the Polish Government had passed on March 31st, and supplemented by the order of October 6th. With the Grynszpans, 484 persons were arrested in Hanover and deported to Poland.

'We were not offered an explanation,' Sendel Grynszpan related.[3]

It was a Thursday, October 27th 1938. A policeman knocked on our door and told us to report to the police station with our passports. He said, 'Don't bother to take anything else, you'll be right back.' When we reached the police station, my wife, my daughter, my son Marcus and myself, we saw a number of people sitting or standing. Some were weeping. The police inspector was shouting at the top of his voice, 'Sign here. You are being deported.' I had to sign like everyone else. We were taken to the concert hall beside the Leine, where about 600 people had been assembled from various parts of Hanover. We were kept there for about 24 hours until Friday night, when police vans took us, about twenty at a time, to the station. The streets of Hanover teemed with people shouting, 'Send the Jews to Palestine'.

We were taken by train to the German border station at Neu Bentschen on the line connecting Frankfurt an Oder with Posen. We arrived at about 6 o'clock on Saturday morning. There were

trains from all over Germany: Leipzig, Berlin, Cologne, Düsseldorf, Bielefeld, Essen, Bremen. We were about 12,000 in all. That
was Saturday, October 29th. When we got to the border we were
searched. We were only allowed to take 10 marks; any excess
was confiscated. That was German law, we were told: 'You
didn't have more than that when you arrived in Germany and you
can't take any more away with you now.' We were kept under
guard and not allowed to communicate with anyone. The SS told
us we would have to walk about 2 kilometres to the border. Those
who couldn't walk were beaten until the road was wet with their
blood. Their baggage was taken away. We were dealt with cruelly
and barbarously. It was the first time that I realized how barbarous
the Germans really are. They made us run while they shouted,
'Run! Run!' I was struck down at the roadside, but my son
Marcus took me by the hand and said, 'Come on, Papa, run.
They'll kill you if you don't.'

Finally we reached the border. We crossed it. The women went
first because they began firing at us. The Poles had no idea why
we were there or why there were so many of us. A Polish general
and some officers came to examine our papers. They saw that we
were all Polish citizens – we had special passports and they decided
to let us into Poland.

We were taken to a tiny village of 6,000 inhabitants, although
there were 12,000 of us. It was raining hard. There were a number
of old people among us, some of whom fell or fainted; others
had heart attacks. Although we hadn't eaten since Thursday evening and were very hungry, we did not want to eat the Germans'
bread. We were taken to the stables of a military camp as there
was no room anywhere else. We didn't write immediately because
we were too hungry. On Sunday a truck came from Poznan and
we all rushed round it. They threw bread and those who managed
to catch any had bread, but it turned out that there was enough
bread for all of us. Then I wrote a letter to my son Herschel in
Paris. It told him not to write to us in Germany but to Zbonszyn
in Poland.

This was the letter sent by his daughter Berta. It reached Herschel Grynszpan in Paris on November 3rd.

Born in the aftermath of the First World War, Grynszpan experienced a childhood which was as turbulent as the times in which he lived. He was refused by a nursery school, and attended the municipal school in Hanover from 1926 until 1935 without completing his last year. He did not lack ability but he was not an enthusiastic pupil. His teachers regarded him as unusually intelligent, but he was unruly and truculent. His Jewish friends, who learned to be chary of his blows, called him Judas Maccabaeus. He had no gentile friends.

After leaving the municipal school in 1935, Grynszpan, who had in the meantime become a member of Mizrahi, a Zionist religious organization in Hanover, went on May 10th 1935 to study Hebrew at the Yashiva Salomon Breuer (Higher Talmudic School) in Frankfurt am Main. His aim was to emigrate to Palestine. He returned to his family in Hanover on April 15th 1936. When his brother Marcus became apprenticed to a Jewish plumber in Hanover, Grynszpan decided to visit an aunt in Brussels, where he hoped to obtain a visa for Palestine.

As a German-born Pole, Grynszpan had been granted a passport valid for two years by the Polish Consul General in Hamburg on June 3rd 1935. In order to obtain a Belgian visa, he had to request a re-entry permit from the German police in Hanover. He requested one on July 8th 1936, and on the 16th was granted a permit valid until October 1st 1937. Until then Grynszpan had always intended to emigrate to Palestine, but a meeting changed the course of his life.

'One day,' he explained, 'I saw an old man at the synagogue who told me it was difficult to find young men like me who respected books. He asked me to go and see him. He was an old watchmaker. I didn't like talking to strangers but I accepted his invitation. He advised me not to stay in Germany. "A young man like you mustn't stay in Germany, where Jews are not men but dogs." He suggested that I go to France. When I spoke to my father about it he agreed

37

on the condition that my Uncle Abraham, who lived in Paris, would put me up. I myself wanted to go to Palestine. My father wrote to my uncle, who said he would have me and even offered to adopt me.'

In mid-July 1936 Grynszpan left Hanover for Brussels, carrying a valid passport and visa. He seems to have travelled via Essen, where he spent two or three weeks with his Uncle Isaac. In Brussels he went to his Uncle Wolf at 37 Rue des Tanneries, but his uncle was less than pleased to see him when he found out that he was penniless. Put off by his icy reception at the hands of his Uncle Wolf, Grynszpan went to stay with a neighbour, Zaslawsky, who was also remotely related to him. This charitable neighbour, however, cautioned young Grynszpan that his stay must be brief.

On September 15th Mme Rosenthal, Zaslawsky's sister, who lived in Rue Vilain in Paris, arrived in Brussels. When she left a few days later to return to Paris, Grynszpan accompanied her. They travelled together to the Franco-Belgian border, which Grynszpan then crossed in secret by taking a tram which was reserved for railway employees and not checked at the border. He thus arrived at Valenciennes in France.

Grynszpan's situation had now changed. In Quiévrain, on the Belgian side of the Franco–Belgian frontier, he was acting legally: his German papers were in order until June 3rd 1937. But in Valenciennes, on the French side of the border, his actions became illicit and stealthy. He had entered France without a visa or visitor's permit.

He reached his Uncle Abraham at his Parisian home at 23 Boulevard Richard Lenoir towards the end of September 1936. From then until August 1938 Grynszpan struggled to put his papers in order.

'Soon after his arrival,' Abraham related, 'I took him to the Central Committee for Assistance to Jewish Emigrés at 5 Rue de la Durance, where they immediately prepared an application for an identity card which I signed. The application was sent on my behalf to the Minister of the Interior. I also consulted police headquarters, where I presented Herschel's passport. As he had no visa I had to pay a fine of 100 francs and I signed a guaranty undertaking to support him and to teach him a trade.'

The Central Committee for Assistance to Jewish Emigrés did not present the identity card application to the Minister of the Interior until January 29th 1937. The Minister received it a fortnight later and forwarded it to police headquarters on February 20th. Grynszpan was given a receipt which served as a residence permit.

On May 24th 1937, when his re-entry visa to return to Germany was about to expire, Grynszpan requested a duplicate passport from the Polish Consulate in Paris. He claimed to have lost his passport a few days before. Early in August the Consulate granted a passport, which was valid for six months, until February 7th 1938. In the meantime, his German re-entry permit and his residence permit at Hanover both expired. Neither Grynszpan nor his father tried to extend either of them. And nothing was done to renew the duplicate passport when it expired on February 7th 1938. The illicit refugee had consequently made legal residence impossible for himself in four countries at once: France, Belgium, Poland and Germany.

In Paris, Grynszpan led a leisurely life of pleasurable pastimes rather than work. Very occasionally he would help his uncle by running errands for his confectioner's shop. He was given 30 or 40 francs pocket money weekly. He did not like staying at home and went out whenever there was an opportunity for amusement. After his difficult years in Hanover, Paris life was like a dream. He often joined outings organized by sports clubs or by the Jewish newspapers, or attended afternoon dances at the town hall in the Third Arrondissement. His best friend at that time was probably Nathan Kaufman, a neighbour. Kaufman and Grynszpan often met at Uncle Abraham's home. Although their families were neighbours and practised the same trade, they only saw one another occasionally.

On August 11th 1938 Grynszpan received a ministerial order to leave French territory within four days. Although there was the hope that he might be granted a renewal of his Polish passport, he listened to bad advice and decided to remain in France illegally. His uncle was obliged to hide him in a servant's room on the fifth floor at 8 Rue Martel.

Grynszpan intended to apply again to the Minister of Foreign Affairs for a residence permit and an identity card, but after Thursday, November 3rd, when news of his family's plight in Germany reached him in the letter from his sister Berta, he forgot his own situation. A single thought obsessed him : to take vengeance on the Germans for his family's persecution. This obsession grew more consuming as he read the reports published in the Yiddish daily paper, *Pariser Haint* ('*Parisian Day*'), which his uncle received. One article in the issue of November 4th by the paper's correspondent at Zbonszyn gave a vivid account of what had happened to the deported Jews :

'Critical situation of Polish Jews deported from Germany. More than 8,000 persons have overnight been rendered stateless. They were rounded up and deported, largely to Zbonszyn, in a no-man's land between Germany and Poland. Their living conditions are uncomfortable and distressing. 1,200 of them have fallen ill and several hundreds are without shelter. As there is a risk of epidemic, Red Cross doctors with the help of doctors from the OSE (Oeuvre de Secours aux Enfants) have distributed typhus vaccinations and 10,000 aspirin tablets. A number of instances of insanity and suicide have been recorded.'

Throughout Saturday, November 5th, Grynszpan's thoughts returned with feverish anxiety to the events at Zbonszyn. What had happened was horrible. He had not decided precisely how, but somehow the Germans, who were responsible, must be punished.

The following day, in high agitation, he reproached his uncle and his aunt for not being sufficiently concerned about his family. His uncle was irritated. 'If you don't like it here you can leave.' Grynszpan was about to go, but his aunt and his friend Nathan Kaufman dissuaded him. Then the argument between Abraham and his nephew sharpened; Grynszpan lost his temper and stalked out, slamming the door. Kaufman followed and accompanied him to a dance at the Aurore sports club.

The two friends left the dance at about half-past seven that evening. They agreed to meet again at a restaurant called Tout Va Bien in Boulevard de Strasbourg at about nine o'clock. Kaufman found himself waiting in vain. When he realized that Grynszpan had let him down he returned home. Abraham grew concerned at his nephew's delay in returning and went looking for him at Kaufman's house. While they were debating what might have happened, Grysnzpan was busy with other plans, under the spell of a compelling idea which had first occurred to him that afternoon. As he and Kaufman were passing through the Saint Martin district on their way to the dance, a gunsmith's shop window had caught his eye and answered the question which he had been brooding over since the previous day. A gun. Kill.

A swarm of images invaded his thoughts. I'll buy a gun: I'll go to the embassy. I'll ask to see the Ambassador. I'll be shown in. I'll aim my gun at him and shout, 'Vengeance for the Polish Jews.' I'll shoot him down like a dog.

Grynszpan was careful not to share these thoughts with Kaufman. He agreed to meet him knowing that he would not keep the appointment. When they parted at the metro station at Strasbourg-Saint Denis at half-past seven, Grynszpan went to the nearest hotel, the Hotel de Suez, near the Scala cinema, and asked for a room. He signed the register under the name of Heinrich Halter, salesman from Hanover. He did not fill in the green card required for foreigners, claiming that he had left his documents with his bags at the station. He would complete the formalities when he had collected his luggage. He paid in advance. He was handed the key and he went up to his room. He did not emerge until the following morning. After a restless night, disturbed by visions of his unfortunate parents, he wrote them a farewell message on the back of a photograph of himself. At about eight o'clock that morning he ordered breakfast and, curiously enough, paid for it at once. Half an hour later he left the hotel and headed straight for a shop called 'The Sharp Blade' at 61 Rue du Faubourg Saint Martin. M. Carpe served him. On his request for a revolver, the gunsmith showed him a wide selection of firearms. Grynszpan did not know whether to choose an automatic or a small-barrel pistol.

'Why do you need the gun?' the gunsmith asked him.

'I am a foreigner,' Grynszpan replied, 'and I have to carry large amounts of money for my father.'

M. Carpe advised him to take a small-barrel 6.35 calibre pistol as it was easier to handle than an automatic. Grynszpan agreed and asked how it worked. After paying 245 francs for gun and ammunition and showing his Polish passport, he left the shop and headed for the Tout Va Bien restaurant. He reached it at nine o'clock and went directly to the toilet, loaded the pistol with five bullets and slipped it into the left inside pocket of his jacket. After visiting the bar he left the restaurant and descended into the Metro at Strasbourg-Saint Denis station. He changed trains at Madeleine and alighted at Solférino, the station nearest the German embassy. A few minutes after his arrival Grynszpan was shown into Third Secretary Ernst vom Rath's office. Vom Rath, sitting at his desk, signalled Grynszpan to come in and offered him a seat in the left-hand armchair. Vom Rath asked what he wanted. 'Did you have an important document to give me?'

Grynszpan rose, pulled out the gun from his inside jacket pocket and levelled it at vom Rath, crying, 'You are a filthy boche and here, in the name of twelve thousand persecuted Jews, is your document.'

Grynszpan fired five times at Ernst vom Rath. Although grievously wounded, vom Rath found the strength to drag himself to the door, calling for help.

The porters, Nagorka and Krüger, reached the scene of the crime first. They found Grynszpan standing motionless in the office, having made no attempt to escape. They seized him and handed him over to Officer François Autret, the policeman on guard outside the embassy, who escorted him to the police station in Rue de Bourgogne. Ernst vom Rath, gravely wounded but still conscious, was carried to the Alma Clinic at 166 Rue de l'Université. He was able to relate to Achenbach, the First Secretary of the Embassy, that the visitor had fired on him almost the moment he entered his office, shouting that he wanted to avenge the Jews.

Grynszpan's was not the first attempt by a Jew on the life of a Nazi official. Nearly three years before, on February 4th 1936, Wilhelm Gustloff, the head of the National Socialist organization of Germans resident in Switzerland, had been assassinated at his home in Davos by David Frankfurter, a Jewish Yugoslav student who had taken refuge in Switzerland after Hitler seized power. 'As to my reason for killing Gustloff,' Frankfurter is reported to have said after his arrest, 'I shall tell you what happened. I was seized by uncontrollable hatred for all brown shirts or Nazis.'[4]

Even if, unlike Gustloff, the embassy secretary vom Rath did not at first glance appear to embody the qualities of a fanatically un-scrupulous Nazi, and was subsequently dismissed as an adversary of National Socialism ill regarded by his superiors in the NSDAP, he was the son of a Prussian aristocrat and joined the Nazi Party long before Hitler rose to power.

Ernst Edward vom Rath was born on June 3rd 1909 at Frankfurt am Main. His father was then attached to the Cologne police. On completing secondary school, Ernst enrolled at the University of Bonn, then at the University of Munich and finally at Koenigsberg, the capital of Prussia. In 1932, after successfully sitting for his law examinations, he was admitted as a trainee at the bailiff's court at Zinter, near Koenigsberg, after which he served as chief clerk in the Berlin magistrate's court. Then he decided to embark on a diplo-matic career, beginning as junior civil servant at the Foreign Ministry in Berlin in 1934. The following year he passed the competitive diplomatic examinations and, after a term in the Foreign Ministry in Berlin, was sent to the German Embassy in Paris as personal secretary to Ambassador Koester, his uncle. After a second six-month stint in Berlin, he was assigned to the German consul general at Calcutta. Here his health was seriously undermined by dysentery. As the consulate was short-staffed, he struggled to remain at his post until his doctors finally ordered him to return to Germany. He spent four months in a sanatorium at Saint-Blasien in the

Black Forest. After his recovery he was sent once more to Paris in July 1938 to take up the post of Third Secretary at the German Embassy.[5]

Carried to the Alma Clinic only a few minutes after the shooting, vom Rath was placed in the care of Professor Baumgartner, the father of the future minister and governor of the Bank of France. Vom Rath had been hit by only two of the five bullets fired by Grynszpan. One, lodged in his shoulder, was easily removed. The other had entered his groin on the left side, ripped through his spleen, grazed his stomach and had finally lodged in his left lung. Professor Baumgartner operated to remove his spleen and suture his stomach in two places. According to the surgeon, it was the wounds sustained from the second bullet which would prove crucial.

In the meantime, the German Ambassador to France, Count von Welczeck, rushed to the Quai d'Orsay to demand a meeting with the French Foreign Minister, Georges Bonnet. Bonnet received him at once. The Ambassador informed him of the attempt on his Third Secretary's life, and Bonnet immediately expressed his regrets and asked von Welczeck to convey them to his government. The Prime Minister, Edouard Daladier, readily agreed to do as much again later the same day. As soon as Hitler heard of the attempt from the German Foreign Ministry he promoted vom Rath to the rank of Embassy Counsellor and ordered his own personal physical, Karl Brandt, to go to Paris with Professor Georg Magnus of Munich.

The Führer's medical emissaries left Nuremberg at 1.44 in the morning of November 8th aboard a three-motor Junker. After stopping briefly in Cologne they arrived at Le Bourget in Paris at five o'clock and were greeted at the airport by Breuer, German Embassy Counsellor. It was still early in the morning when they reached the Alma Clinic. After a lengthy and careful examination of vom Rath they published the following bulletin: 'The condition of Counsellor vom Rath is regarded as serious in view of the wound in the stomach. Considerable loss of blood, due to the laceration of the patient's spleen, has been treated with transfusions. The excellent surgical and medical treatment administered by Professor Baumgartner of Paris allows us to hope for an improvement.'[6]

Early in the afternoon of the same day, a second blood transfusion produced a slight improvement in the patient's condition. In this dramatic context, advocates of Franco-German friendship drew comfort from the fact that the blood-donor, M. Thomas, who had given blood 107 times previously, was a French veteran of the First World War and had been awarded the Croix de Guerre.

During the course of the day Count von Welczeck reported to the Foreign Minister in Berlin, emphasizing the uniform 'neutrality' of the French press, with the exceptions of the Communist paper *Humanité,* the 'crypto-communist' *Ce Soir,* edited by Louis Aragon, *L'Oeuvre* of Marcel Déat, and the press agency Havas. Havas had reported on November 7th:

'With regard to the attack on M. vom Rath of the German Embassy, 78 Rue de Lille, the Press Attaché of the Embassy has issued the following statement to the press:

"A young man, almost an adolescent, who was among the first visitors to the German Embassy this morning, asked to see the Ambassador's secretary in order to deliver an important document. He was admitted to the office of a young attaché at the Embassy, M. vom Rath, nephew of former Ambassador Koester, for a long time representative of the Third Reich in France." '[7]

This version of the incident vexed the Ambassador's staff, who found it too innocuous and imprecise. Havas therefore published a second statement five minutes later in which the 'young man, almost an adolescent' became a 'murderer in full possession of his faculties and a fanatic who with malice and aforethought sought vengeance for the Polish Jews deported from Germany.'[8]

Among the newspapers which did not espouse the 'neutrality' which the German Ambassador had praised, *L'Oeuvre* published an article signed by Paul Elbel disapproving of the assassination but commenting that 'the head of the press section at the German Embassy has explained the motivation of the crime in a manner which would not be acceptable to everyone'. The article concluded

'Like it or not, the persecution of the Jews, and the antisemitism which has been unleashed throughout Germany, have turned this young man into a murderer.'[9]

At about 9.30 on the morning of November 9th M. Thomas was summoned for a third blood transfusion. Vom Rath had slept restlessly. His parents had arrived on the North Express from Cologne and were anxious to hear the clinic's prognosis.

Professor Baumgartner gave up hope of saving vom Rath a little before noon. When it was suggested that vom Rath's youth might aid his chances, the surgeon expressed pessimism because vom Rath had been wounded in three places.

Vom Rath lapsed into a coma at about three o'clock in the afternoon. Later the German Embassy issued a statement: 'M. vom Rath, recently appointed Embassy Counsellor by the Führer, died at 4.30 this afternoon of wounds sustained from the attempt on his life of November 7th.'

Half an hour later, Dr Paul, a forensic doctor from the Court of the Seine, arrived at the clinic to examine the body. At half-past ten the coffin was loaded on to a hearse attended by nearly two hundred members of the German community in Paris. The procession was led by Count von Welczeck and the doctors who had been sent from Berlin. Three days later a memorial service was held at the Lutheran Church in Rue Blanche. Bonnet attended the ceremony personally, while Daladier was represented by his principal private secretary, M. Chataigneau, and the President of France, Albert Lebrun, was represented by Colonel Tassi. M. Dahlgrün, the priest who conducted the service, and Hitler's representative, Baron von Weiszäcker, both spoke about vom Rath's career without alluding to the political issues involved in his death. Vom Rath's mortal remains were taken to the frontier station at Aix-la-Chapelle on Wednesday, November 16th. A special German train then bore them as far as Düsseldorf. At the stations and along the entire route of the train National Socialist Party ranks lined the tracks. In Düsseldorf the diplomat's body was placed in the Rheinhalle. The walls of the hall were draped alternately in black and National Socialist colours.

The coffin was covered in a German flag and encircled with wreaths of white chysanthemums. The simple wreath of fronds crossed by the German national colours given by Hitler was propped against the front of the coffin. Beside it the counsellor's decorations were displayed on a velvet cushion. Among the many wreaths were those of von Ribbentrop, the Führer's heir-apparent Rudolf Hess, the Italian Foreign Minister Count Ciano, and Georges Bonnet. One member each of the SA, the SS, the Hitler Youth and the National Socialist Motor Corps stood guard with ritualistic solemnity around the podium on which the coffin was displayed. From early in the morning thousands filed past it, raising rigid arms in final salutes.[10]

Hitler arrived in Düsseldorf and proceeded directly to the Rhein-halle. Those present saluted him as he entered. The Chancellor and von Ribbentrop paused together for a moment before the coffin and then sat in the front row of the audience. Beethoven's Heroic March was played; then followed a speech by Bohle, the Secretary of State and head of the Nazi organizations of Germans abroad. 'The deaths of W. Gustloff and vom Rath place a solemn obligation on every German living abroad, regardless of his circumstances, faithfully to serve his Führer and the German fatherland.' Then von Ribbentrop gave a funeral oration recalling Hitler's words over W. Gustloff's grave three years before. 'We accept the challenge and we know how to respond.'[11] The ceremony finished at 1.45, after the Chancellor had again shaken hands with vom Rath's parents and expressed his condolences.

From the moment he had arrived at the police station in Rue de Bourgogne with Officer Autret, Herschel Grynszpan had struggled to explain his action.

'I fired five shots,' he told Autret, 'at the only man present at the Embassy, to retaliate against the Germans. I wanted to avenge my parents' mis-treatment in Germany.'

Police Inspector Monneret was about to receive the murderer's deposition when he was interrupted by Lorz, an official from the

Embassy sent by Count von Welczeck, requesting permission to attend the preliminary interrogation. Contrary to the rules of criminal procedure, as was later emphasized by the Criminal Investigation Department, the Inspector not only granted the request, but allowed the Nazi envoy actually to conduct the interrogation.

'Why did you shoot the Embassy secretary?' asked Lorz in French.

'To avenge persecutions by the filthy Germans,' Grynszpan replied with exasperation.

'Why did you feel it was your duty to do this?' Lorz pressed.

'Because the deported Poles are of my religion.'

'Are you Jewish?'

'Yes.'[12]

The farewell card which Grynszpan had written in his room at the Hotel de Suez was found on him; it was seen to corroborate his explanation:

My dear parents. I could not do otherwise. May God forgive me. My heart bleeds at the news of 12,000 Jews' suffering. I must protest in such a way that the world will hear me. I must do it. Forgive me. Herschel.

This note was later held by the plaintiff in the civil case (namely, the Reich) as evidence of premeditation.

After hearing Grynszpan's first confession, Inspector Monneret proceeded to reconstruct the crime. Late in the afternoon he escorted Grynszpan along the path which he had followed since the previous evening. He confronted Grynszpan with his Uncle Abraham, the receptionist at the Hotel de Suez, and the gunsmith Carpe. Grynszpan refused to enter the German Embassy for fear of being trapped by the Nazis. The Inspector went alone to the scene of the crime. That evening he made a verbal report of his first interrogation to the Criminal Investigation Department, stating that Grynszpan had confessed to the crime by which he claimed to have avenged the German Jews.

Grynszpan was escorted to the Criminal Investigation Department just before midnight. Here his second interrogation was conducted by

Police Inspector Badin. Grynszpan confessed that after receiving his sister's post-card he had resolved to commit an act of vengeance against an official of the Reich. Later, during the judicial enquiry, he asked to withdraw this statement, made under the influence of stress and fatigue.

In the mid-afternoon of the following day, November 8th, three criminal investigators escorted Grynszpan to the Public Prosecutor's office. His right hand was manacled, while one of the officers firmly gripped his left. His ashen face and small, frail body conveyed his sense of bewilderment. Szwarc and Vesinne-Larue, the lawyers engaged by the Grynszpan family to defend him, had been kept waiting at the Public Prosecutor's office since ten o'clock. They accompanied him to the office of the examining magistrate, Tesnière, where the criminal investigators were replaced by the Republican Guard. Eager to erase the bad impression that he may have given during the earlier questioning Grynszpan said : 'I was not motivated by hatred or by vegeance but by love for my father and my people, who have endured unbearable suffering. I deeply regret having injured anyone, but I had no other way of expressing myself.'

After describing the nightmare lived by Polish Jews in Germany, he added, 'To be Jewish is not a crime. We are not animals. The Jewish people have a right to live.'

Grynszpan was accused of attempted murder by Judge Tesnière, and, two days later, of premeditated murder. In his cell at the Fresnes Prison, he became the centre of a legal hurricane. On the advice of the World Jewish Congress and the Federation of Jewish Societies in France, Grynszpan's uncle, Salomon Grynszpan, dismissed his nephew's lawyers and on November 10th engaged Vincent de Moro-Giafferi (with Weill-Goudchaux and Fränkel, of whom the latter knew Yiddish) to defend Grynszpan.

De Moro-Giafferi found a valuable ally in Mrs Dorothy Thompson of the *New York Herald Tribune,* in obtaining contributions towards the heavy expenses incurred by the defence. She devoted her journalistic skills to marshalling American public opinion behind Grynszpan and the German Jews and broadcast an appeal on Grynszpan's behalf which was heard all over the United States.[13] She received three thousand telegrams, mountains of letters, and hundreds of dollars in cheques although she had not asked for money. Almost everyone offered to help.

A number of American journalists joined her campaign to raise money for Grynszpan's defence. Donations were entrusted to de Moro-Giafferi, who had not only to defend Grynszpan but his Uncle Abraham and his Aunt Chawa as well. After the attempted murder, the police searched their home, arrested them and brought them before the Public Prosecutor. They were charged under Article 4 of a decree regarding foreigners, which stated, 'anyone who aids or abets, whether directly or indirectly, or attempts to aid or abet the illegal entry, transit or residence of a foreigner shall be punished according to the provisions . . .'

After vom Rath's death they were charged with complicity in murder. Judge Tesnière wished to avoid adverse publicity. He realized that he was dealing with people of modest means and pressed for an early trial. At the end of November Abraham and Chawa Grynszpan appeared before the Seventeenth Division of the Civil Court of the Seine. De Moro-Giafferi defended them. Despite efforts to conduct the trial discreetly, some twenty lawyers attended De Moro-Giafferi's performance.

After a feeble case had been presented by the Public Prosecutor, who closed with a demand for heavy sentences, De Moro-Giafferi spoke for over an hour. Turning to face Abraham Grynszpan, de Moro-Giafferi explained that under Article 11 of the decree regarding foreigners, Herschel Grynszpan could not be expelled. 'This article says, "a foreigner who is proven to be unable to leave the country shall not be subject to the provisions of Articles 8 and 9 of this Decree." Now it is obvious that Herschel was unable to return either to Germany or to Poland.'

The court did not accept this argument and sentenced the Grynszpans to four months' imprisonment and a fine of 100 francs. On appeal the sentence was increased to six months' imprisonment for Abraham and reduced to three for his wife.

The German Embassy official who attended the trial described his impressions of De Moro-Giafferi's speech in a report to Count von Welczeck. 'De Moro-Giafferi's power of oratory fascinated the court. He spoke of the "child" Grynszpan rather than of a "murderer". At first he studiously avoided any reference to political matters. But at the end of his plea he could not restrain himself and exclaimed that we should remember the monument to the man who assassinated Austrian Chancellor Dollfuss.'

The German authorities knew De Moro-Giafferi to be not only a skilful lawyer but also an implacable enemy of fascism, and at the news that he had been chosen to conduct Grynszpan's defence they could not conceal their annoyance and dismay. An article in Goebbels' Berlin newspaper *Der Angriff* was headlined VINCENT DE MORO-GIAFFERI DEFENDS WORLD JEWRY.[14] In the months that followed the Nazis resorted to every possible device in an attempt to prove his Jewish descent, but finally conceded that his family tree was 'pure'. The German authorities were further nettled because De Moro-Giafferi, as Radical Party deputy from Corsica and Under Secretary of State for national education in Edouard Herriot's cabinet, had frequently averred his determination to fight Hitler's regime. During the trial resulting from the Reichstag Fire in 1933, he offered his services to an anti-Fascist committee. On Armistice Day, November 11th 1933, he vehemently attacked Hitler and Goering at the Wagram Hall in Paris, accusing them of being the real arsonists. Soon afterwards he became an active member of a committee set up to defend the German communist leader Ernst Thälmann. In 1936, at a conference in Paris on the Nazi system of justice, he appealed to the audience to oppose Nazi injustice.

In the same year De Moro-Giafferi agreed to defend David Frankfurter, the young Jew mentioned above on page 43, who, like Grynszpan, had also murdered a Nazi official. At the trial at Coire in Switzerland, De Moro-Giafferi had claimed extenuating circumstances under the law of Grisons, on the grounds that the young defendant had been actuated by reasonable indignation at the German measures against the Jews.

Despite his skill and his political acumen, which represented a keenly felt threat to the Nazis, De Moro-Giafferi's task in defending Grynszpan was not likely to be easy. The French psychiatric consultants[15] to the Civil Court of the Seine, who were instructed by Tesnière to examine Grynszpan, concluded that he was completely responsible for his actions. 'Within the terms of strictly psychiatric considerations,' their report states, 'we found no pathological symptoms which could support a claim of diminished responsibility for psychological reasons. The young man, Herschel Grynszpan, was not medically insane under the definition in Article 64 of the Criminal Code at the moment when he committed the crime. He is of normal intelligence. In fact, he exhibits some mental subtlety and is not abnormally impressionable. His assessment of certain situations reveals great acuity; for example, when we asked him why he had not preferred to commit suicide, he replied that in our day and age the death of a Jew would not have attracted attention and that his protest would therefore have failed.'[16]

As plaintiff in the civil case, the Reich was initially represented by the German Embassy lawyer. For openly political reasons, he was now replaced by Friedrich Grimm, a lawyer and an agent of Goebbels' Propaganda Services. Grimm, in turn, appointed the French lawyers Maurice Garçon and Maurice Loncle to collaborate in preparing the civil case. Counsellor Wolfgang Diewerge, to whom Goebbels personally assigned the task of following the Grynszpan case, sent a secret message informing Goebbels that De Moro-Giafferi was planning to bring Grynszpan's parents from Poland to testify at the trial. Pressure was immediately put on the Polish government to forbid Grynszpan's parents from leaving Polish territory. Grimm suspected that a first-hand account of their deportation would have a dramatic effect at the trial and prepared a more cheerful version in which, according to the Germans, the Jews' journey was undertaken in the best possible conditions.

'The Polish Jews resident in Hanover,' states the specially prepared report of the Hanover police, were first assembled by sex in two separate dining-rooms in a large restaurant called the Rusthaus at 30 Burgstrasse, very near the home of Grynszpan's relatives at 36 Burgstrasse. Food was provided by the police catering staff and by Secour d'Hiver Israélite [Jewish Winter Aid organization]. Each person was given sufficient food for the journey. The old and the ill were excluded from deportation. Similarly, anyone who had lost his Polish citizenship or who lacked a valid Polish passport was allowed to stay. The police officers and members of the SS were careful to deal fairly with the Jews whom they had been ordered to deport. They even helped, wherever possible, to carry their vast quantities of luggage. No complaints were lodged. The two halls in the Rusthaus, where the Polish Jews resident in Hanover were assembled before their departure for the frontier, were well ventilated and heated. A nurse was permanently on duty in the women's hall, a Red Cross male nurse in the men's hall. A police doctor was also on call. So much food was supplied that after the Jews left, there was enough bread and other foods to provision the same number of persons over again. . . . There was so much to eat, in fact, because many Jews refused what the police offered on the grounds that it was not Kosher and they preferred the food which arrived from the Jewish kitchen.[17]

Friedrich Grimm planned to use the Grynszpan trial as a springboard for Nazi policies. He gave his French colleagues all the legal and antisemitic propaganda material that he could find.

The Nazis had not waited for Counsellor vom Rath's murder to disseminate Nazi propaganda in France. In 1929, four years before Hitler's rise to power, a handful of his dedicated supporters established a Paris section of the National Socialist Party. By the time of vom Rath's murder they comprised six hundred members, organized with Prussian discipline. They were thoroughly familiar with Parisian society, spoke fluent French and could claim ties of friendship with France. They broadcast Nazi propaganda to the German colony in France and to anyone who upheld German fascism. Their indirect

propaganda was more insidious, consisting of articles and announce-
ments in the French press, and pamphlets and books published at
the expense of Dr Goebbels' propaganda services.

According to a pamphlet published at this time by *Le Petit
Parisien*,[18] more than twenty supposedly French newspapers and
magazines were disseminating Nazi ideas. Patriotic associations in
Paris, such as Le Réveil Français at 54 Rue Saint Lazare, or Le
Faisceau Français at 31 Avenue de l'Opera, distributed fifty thousand
pamphlets and posted three thousand large notices urging the French
people to rid themselves of the foreigners and Jews in their midst.
The printers' bills were paid directly by the German Ministry of
Propaganda.[19]

Before Gustav vom Rath, the victim's father, gave his testimony,
Grimm arranged a meeting with Maurice Garçon, who was acting for
the plaintiff and Diewerge, the propaganda consultant. He also held
a press conference with Diewerge's assistance at which they asked
the German journalists in Paris to give maximum coverage to Gustav
vom Rath's arrival.

While vom Rath's father was being heard by the examining
magistrate, one of the plaintiff's lawyers, Garçon, objected to the
interpreter on the grounds that he was Jewish. Friedrich Grimm was
proposed as a substitute and Judge Tesnière agreed without pausing
to consider the legality of such a choice. The press release on the
ensuing examination which Havas Agency issued was written by
Germans. It was printed in its entirety by the French press with
accompanying photographs. Grimm and Diewerge were pleased to
find Judge Tesnière responsive to the German point of view.

'Judge Tesnière,' commented Friedrich Grimm in a report to
Goebbels[20] after one of his innumerable visits to Paris, 'makes no
attempt to conceal his irritation at the barrage of messages from
Grynszpan and his family. He reckons that the further north one goes
the more truthful the people, and the further south – towards the
Mediterranean, Italy, Spain – the less people adhere to what is true,
particularly the Jews in the East.'

In January 1939 Friedrich Grimm determined that the state of

Franco-German relations was propitious, and with the support of Heydrich, the head of the Reich Intelligence, he began pressing for the trial to open. When the Germans invaded Czechoslovakia two months later French opinion was reversed. Now Chief Counsel for the defence pressed for an early start, while Grimm, sensing that the atmosphere favoured Grynszpan's acquittal, stalled for time. Again the trial was postponed. From month to month political events repeatedly intervened, until the invasion of Poland and France's subsequent declaration of war against the Reich seriously obstructed the start of the trial.

3

The Kill

When news of vom Rath's assassination reached Germany the Jewish communities realized what would be in store for them.

On November 7th the German press relegated the incident to a few lines on the second page, but the following day they blazoned it across the front pages, gave increased space to the 'world Jewish conspiracy' and foretold the exaction of severe reprisals. The most moderate daily, the *Deutsche Allgemeine Zeitung,* announced in its Berlin edition of November 8th: 'The Jewish attempt against the German Embassy in Paris will have, as everyone now knows, the most serious repercussions on the Jews, including foreign Jews living in our country. They will learn to their cost that the assassin's phrase 'racial brother' cuts both ways.' Goebbels' *Völkischer Beobachter* did not trifle with circumlocutions. 'It is clear,' the edition of the same day stated, 'what conclusions the Germans will draw from this latest event. We shall no longer tolerate the hundreds of thousands of Jews within our territory who control entire streets of shops, who avail themselves of our public entertainments, and as foreign landlords pocket the wealth of German leaseholders while their brothers in religion incite war on Germany and assassinate German officials.' Other newspapers[1] reported with satisfaction the antisemitic comments published in such French papers as *La Nation, Le Jour, Le Journal* and *L'Action Française.*

The government ominously forbade publication of Jewish newspapers in Germany after November 8th, thus outlawing three large newspapers, the *Central Verein Zeitung* (with a circulation of 40,000 copies), the *Judische Rundschau* (circulation 26,000) and the *Israelitisches Wochenblatt* (circulation 25,000), as well as the four cultural papers, the sports magazines, and specialist magazines, not to mention the twenty-five community bulletins (the circulation of the Berlin bulletin alone was 40,000). In this way, the government lopped off the last source of information and communication available to the Jews, who had already been ostracized from public life and deprived of their radios.

A series of antisemitic demonstrations on November 8th all traced a similar pattern in a large number of places. The heads of local Party organizations held meetings to denounce 'Jewish crimes', after which the local synagogues were set on fire, and Jewish shops and homes were pillaged and wrecked. The following morning Nazi officials visited the cities and villages in which no demonstrations had occurred to urge the local Party leaders to organize action against the Jews. On the same day the Nazis harassed many of the Jews who went to the French Travel Office in the famous street Unter den Linden in Berlin to purchase tickets to leave the country.[2]

Magnus Davidsohn, reader of the principal synagogue in Berlin, paid a visit with his wife to Counsellor vom Rath's parents, who happened to be neighbours and acquaintances of many years' standing. When he expressed his condolences and the sympathy of the Jewish community, Herr vom Rath, distraught with grief, responded 'My dear Reverend, neither you nor any other Jew is responsible for this. I think my son was assassinated on orders. He spoke too much and a hired assassin killed him.' Magnus Davidsohn uselessly tried to explain that the young murderer had sought to revenge his parents' deportation; the old Prussian officer, whom the Nazis later made the figurehead of a department dealing with racial questions, clung obstinately to his own version of what had happened.

On the evening of November 9th, the old Nazi guard gathered at the Munich town hall to celebrate the anniversary of the putsch of 1923. A little after nine o'clock, a messenger brought Hitler the news of vom Rath's death. The Führer, who was visibly moved, signalled to Goebbels. They whispered together for a moment, then the Führer abruptly walked out without giving his speech. As he left he announced, 'The SA should be allowed to have a fling.'[3]

A report on the members of the SA and SS arrested afterwards for murder and other criminal offences committed against the Jews on the night of November 9th–10th was submitted to Marshal Goering by Walter Buch, acting for the Supreme Tribunal of the Nazi Party, on February 13th 1939.[4] In it he pinned the major share of the blame for the pogrom on Dr Goebbels, whose fanatical stories featured the 'spontaneous' antisemitic demonstrations that took place in reaction to the news of Grynszpan's crime. These convinced the leaders of the Nazi Party that they should not appear officially to have authorized the pogrom, although they virtually planned and organized it.

The Minister of Propaganda's fundamental responsibility for unleashing the pogrom was confirmed by Baldur von Schirach, head of the Hitler Youth, Niepolt, Deputy and District Party Leader in Munich, and Obernitz, head of the SA, all of whom testified at the Nuremberg trials that they attended the meeting on the evening of November 9th.[5] It is unlikely that there is any substance in Prince Schaumburg-Lippe's claim that Goebbels was appalled at the extent of the pogrom and blamed Julius Streicher, the malignant District Party Leader in Nuremburg, and 'those idiots in Munich'.[6] It is more probable that on the evening of November 9th Goebbels was acting in accord with a more sweeping strategy designed to expel all the Jews from Germany. As we have seen, this strategy had been mapped out by Hitler and his principal associates early in 1938. Otto Dietrich claimed in his memoirs, *Twelve Years with Hitler*,[7] that Hitler alone was to blame for the pogrom and ordered Goebbels to organize it and to advise the SA how to proceed.

The probability that a general strategy had been hammered out beforehand is reinforced by still another detail. The SA chiefs in Munich returned after their meeting to their hotel, the Rheinischer Hof, at about eleven o'clock to telephone instructions relating to the

pogrom through to their regional sections, but an independent teletype message, signed 'Müller, Gestapo II,' was secretly sent out
from Berlin to all the police headquarters after 11.55 p.m. It reads
as follows:

1. Action will be taken against the Jews, particularly against
their synagogues, throughout Germany at the earliest possible
moment. The police should co-operate with other forces of order
to guard against the possibility of pillaging or other excesses.

2. Any important archives housed in synagogues should be removed to safety immediately.

3. Preparations should be made to arrest between 20,000 and
30,000 Jews throughout the Reich, preference being given to the
wealthier Jews. Further instructions will follow during the course
of the night.

4. In carrying out these instructions any Jews found in possession
of arms will be dealt with extremely severely. The regular and
reserve troops of the SS may be called upon at any time during the
assignment. But overall direction of the operation shall be the
responsibility of the police.[8]

The substance of this message certainly resembled the instructions
which the SA chiefs telephoned to their sections, but there were
several important divergences. Firstly, although the SA instructions
referred to burning synagogues, it was not archives but religious
objects which they ordered to be removed to safety, with the further
recommendation that firemen should not be called in except to
protect neighbouring buildings. Secondly, the SA chiefs expressly
ordered the destruction of shops and the posting of notices on burnt-
out synagogues and other ruined buildings, saying, 'Vengeance for
the Murder of vom Rath,' 'Death to World Jewry,' 'No Alliances
with Countries which are Friends of the Jews'.[9] Thirdly, whereas
Müller's message specifies that Jews carrying arms should be treated
severely, the SA ordered them to be killed. The fourth and most

crucial difference had to do with the way in which responsibility for the operation was distributed. While Müller's message provided for SS participation but assigned overriding responsibility to the police, the SA instructions stated explicitly, 'The Führer does not wish the police to intervene.'

Müller's distribution of command, and his order to arrest twenty to thirty thousand German Jews (which is not mentioned in the SA instructions), seem to suggest that, without notifying his superiors, he was following a prearranged plan activated by vom Rath's death. This seems plausible in the light of a telephone call which the Security Chief, Heydrich, who was staying at the Four Seasons Hotel in Munich, received at about 11.30 p.m. from the chief of police and security in Munich, Baron von Eberstein. Von Eberstein had escorted the Führer to his Munich apartment at about ten o'clock and had then gone to the Odeon Square for a swearing-in ceremony of SS recruits. Here news reached him that a synagogue and the castle belonging to Baron Hirsch had been set ablaze by unidentified persons and that the firemen had been prevented from putting the fires out. Von Eberstein immediately sent the SS to extinguish the fires, restore order and capture the arsonists. He then notified Heydrich and requested instructions.

Heydrich immediately rang Himmler, who needed first to consult Hitler. Heydrich accordingly did not reply with official instructions until 1.20 in the morning, nearly an hour and a half after the Gestapo instructions had been sent out from Berlin. Heydrich's instructions, which were broadcast from Munich, synthesized Müller's plan and the SA orders. They stressed that police operations should be co-ordinated with those of the political services. The police were to take charge of demolition and incendiary operations so as to prevent pillaging and possible damage to neighbouring Aryan property. They were not to interfere in demonstrations but to supervise them in accordance with the orders which they had received. No one was to molest foreigners, including foreign Jews. Archives and documents belonging to the Jewish communities were to be seized by the police and removed to safety with the help of officers of the criminal branch and members of the secret service and the SS. Müller's order to arrest twenty to thirty thousand of the wealthier Jews was clarified. Only healthy men who were not too old were to be arrested. They were not to be treated roughly but transported to concentration camps as quickly as possible.[10] Upon receiving these instructions, the Munich police chief added that the law officers were not to wear uniforms. Dressed in civilian clothing, they were to maintain contact with their Party leaders and to be available to supervise any action decided upon.

But all these instructions were ignored by the SA. Dr Goebbels' fiery harangue had convinced them that the hour of the 'final solution' had come. They considered that they had been asked to whip up a pogrom to a frenzied pitch during the following day.

In his report to Marshal Goering on behalf of the Supreme Tribunal of the Nazi Party, Major Buch described the SA's state of mind on the eve of the 'Crystal Night' :

Among the Nazis who had been in the Party from the beginning, it was a normal practice to give hazy unspecific instructions for any operation which the Party did not wish to appear to instigate. Members acquired the habit of overstepping the bounds of their instructions, just as local leaders were used to interpreting the interests of the Party from allusions, particularly in arranging illegal demonstrations.

When Goebbels suggested that the Party should not organize the demonstrations, the Party chiefs present at the Town Hall meeting took it that the Party should not appear to organize them. And this is what Goebbels meant, since the politicians – or activists – who would play a prominent role in this form of demonstration were naturally Party members and attached to Party organizations. The demonstrations, in fact, could only be organized through the Party.

The phrasing of orders often left much to conjecture. For example, the suggestion that not only Grynszpan but all Jews were responsible for vom Rath's death meant that the German people should take vengeance against all Jews . . . that the operations were undertaken on the Führer's orders, that everyone should load his pistol.

By one o'clock in the morning, the SA and the SS, wearing civilian clothes, had burst into action, before Heydrich and Goebbel's instructions reached the Reich security services and the propaganda sections of the Party. From north to south, the brown-shirted hordes fell on synagogues, community houses, old people's homes, Jewish hospitals, children's homes, private homes and Jewish shops.

Seggermann, the head of the SA group at Lesum, a village outside Bremen, telephoned to ask the mayor, 'This is SA Company 411 group commander Seggermann. Have you received your orders?'

'No. What orders?'

'The SA is on stand-by throughout Germany to carry out reprisals for the shooting of vom Rath. No Jews are to be left in Germany after tonight. Their shops are to be destroyed.'

'And what are they really going to do with the Jews?'

'They are to be wiped out. Do you understand? Wiped out.'

The astonished mayor immediately telephoned the SA commander at Bremen. 'It's Koester here, Mayor Koester from Lesum. I'm sorry to trouble you, but I've just received an order that is so ridiculous that I thought I'd ring to find out if there may have been a mistake.' 'There's no mistake,' was the reply. 'The "Night of the Long Knives" has begun at Bremen. The synagogue has already been set alight.' (Paradoxically, the SA chief called the impending pogrom by the name used for the slaughter of his superiors, notably Captain Roehm, in June 1934.)

The SA at Lesum hurried to recover time wasted. They rushed out to round up the few Jews in the village. A group commanded by Scharführer August Frühling and Rottenführer Bruno Mahlsted burst into the bedroom of Herr and Frau Goldberg, who had been awakened by the hubbub and were waiting, frozen with fear, by their beds.

Frühling approached, pistol in hand. 'I have a difficult mission to perform.'

Frau Goldberg replied calmly, 'Please aim carefully.'

Frühling fired. Mahlstedt shot Herr Goldberg.

Sinasohn, another Jew living at Lesum, was shot in the same way.

Frühling and Mahlstedt, with twenty-four other members of the SS and SA, were tried by the Supreme Tribunal of the Nazi Party. Of the sixteen murders reviewed by the tribunal, the special hearing recognized only three and sentenced the accused to penalties ranging from imprisonment for previous offenders to temporary or permanent suspension from political duties for murder, including, in one case, the murder, 'contrary to orders', of a sixteen-year-old boy. The Supreme Tribunal of the Party classified thirteen other cases, comprising seventeen murders, including those at Lesum, as 'acts committed under orders by a superior,' and asked the Führer in the interests of the Party and the State to prevent action in the criminal courts.

The same pattern emerged elsewhere. In Breslau the principal synagogue in Ohlauerstrasse and the orthodox community buildings burned to the ground while the firemen industriously blocked the near-by streets. Groups of SA, wielding truncheons and iron bars, descended on Jewish shops made conspicuous by a previous ordinance which required Jewish proprietors to write their names across their shop fronts in white letters not less than 25 cm high. First the window of a radio shop was shattered. Then men, brandishing iron clubs, broke into a shop that sold spirits next door and smashed the bottles on the shelves one by one, cheered on by a howling mob. Then it was the turn of a store and a cloth merchant's, their stock being scattered in the street.[11]

In Berlin the pogrom was deferred until two o'clock, while specially trained squads isolated the Jewish buildings, cutting telephone lines, switching off electricity and heating. The police diverted traffic from the affected areas.

Unchecked mobs hurled paving stones through Jewish shop-windows, from which they snatched up any object which could be used as a projectile. Seven large synagogues in the capital were set ablaze. As the huge building in Fasanenstrasse went up in flames, the reader, Davidsohn, ran to save what he could.

'Turn on the hoses,' he cried to the fire chief, who stood dumbly watching the spectacle with his men.

'Get out of here. You'll get yourself killed,' the captain snarled. 'I am afraid I can't help. We've come to protect the neighbouring buildings.'

'For the love of God, let me at least bring out the sacred objects.'

Just then there was a sound of pounding and Wolfsohn, the porter, staggered into the courtyard in bloodstained nightclothes. He had refused to surrender the keys to the sanctuary and the doors had been forced. The 78-stop organ was heaved over a balcony. The bronze candelabra were taken down and the scrolls of the Law and their appointments torn and broken. Rabbinical garments were cut to shreds and prayer books were mutilated. Then the SA and SS commandos drenched the wooden benches in petrol, and fire leapt through the building. Davidsohn vainly tried to enter. At five o'clock, when the fire had subsided to smouldering ashes, the mob began to disperse, the firemen rode off and the man who for twenty-seven years had led the community's prayers bowed to recite the Kaddish, the prayer of the dead, before the smoking rubble.

When he returned home, he found an order to report to the police at eight o'clock. There were gathered the leaders of the congregation, the rabbis, readers and cantors, under SA and SS guard. They were held without food until six o'clock that evening, when Davidsohn and some others were released. The rest were among the ten thousand men aged between sixteen and sixty, mostly students, lawyers, doctors and prominent Jews, taken away to concentration camps.

Some men who had been forewarned left their homes to stay with fatherless families, or to spend the night in the underground, while others hid in outlying forests.

Near by, in Potsdam, a boarding school was broken into and the children were roused from sleep in the middle of the night. The synagogue could not be burned down because it stood next to the central post office and a block of flats. Early in the morning of

November 10th, the Gestapo roused the President of the Jewish congregation. The Potsdam congregation had been founded under a charter of Frederick the Great and was still emblazoned with a Prussian eagle bearing sword and sceptre. The President was taken to the synagogue, which was crowded with men in civilian clothes brandishing various weapons. In their impatience they had forced down the back doors, but their leader was not satisfied and demanded to be taken to the 'holy of holies'.

'That is where we are going,' the President replied, leading them up to the reader's table.

A group of twenty-five men shattered the windows with hand-grenades. They tore down the chandeliers and ravaged the women's gallery with hatchets. The chairs of the President and the rabbi were hacked to pieces. The men ripped up the curtains of the Ark and the scrolls so viciously that their leader, who was not a squeamish soul, ordered them to leave.

In Potsdam two men between the ages of sixteen and sixty were arrested and interned in a concentration camp.[12]

The American Consul in the Saxon city of Leipzig, David H. Buffum, sent the following report on events there to the Consul General in Berlin:

The macabre circumstances that form the subject matter of this report had a fittingly gruesome prelude in Leipzig a few hours before they occurred in the form of rites held on one of the principal squares of the city on the night of November 9, 1938, in commemoration of fallen martyrs to the Nazi cause prior to the political take-over in 1933. To such end apparently anything in the corpse category that could be remotely associated with Nazi martyrdom, had been exhumed. At least five year old remains of those who had been considered rowdyish violators of law and order at the time, had been placed in extravagant coffins; arranged around a colossal, flaming urn on the Altermarkt [Old Market] for purposes of display, and ultimately conveyed amid marching troops, flaring torches and funeral music to the 'Ehrenhain'

Leipzig's National Socialistic burial plot. For this propagandistic ceremony the entire market place had been surrounded with wooden lattice work about ten yards high. This was covered with white cloth to form the background for black swastikas at least five yards high and broad. Flame-spurting urns and gigantic banners completed a Wagnerian ensemble as to pomposity of stage setting; but it cannot be truthfully reported that the ceremony aroused anything akin to awe among the crowds who witnessed it. Judging from a few very guardedly whispered comments, the populace was far more concerned over the wanton waste of materials in these days when textiles of any kind are exceedingly scarce and expensive, rather than being actuated by any particularly reverent emotions. On the other hand for obvious reasons, there were no open manifestations of disapproval. The populace was destined to be much more perturbed the following morning during the course of the most violent debacle the city had probably ever witnessed.

The shattering of shop windows, looting of stores and dwellings of Jews which began in the early hours of November 10, 1938, was hailed subsequently in the Nazi press as 'a spontaneous wave of righteous indignation throughout Germany, as a result of the cowardly Jewish murder of Third Secretary von [sic] Rath in the German Embassy at Paris.' So far as a very high percentage of the German populace is concerned, a state of popular indignation that would spontaneously lead to such excesses, can be considered as nonexistent. On the contrary, in viewing the ruins and attendant measures employed, all of the local crowds observed were obviously benumbed over what had happened and aghast over the unprecedented fury of Nazi acts that had been or were taking place with bewildering rapidity throughout their city. The whole lamentable affair was organized in such a sinister fashion, as to lend credence to the theory that the execution of it had involved studied preparation. It has been ascertained by this office that the plan of 'spontaneous indignation' leaked out in Leipzig several hours before news of the death of Third Secretary von

Rath had been broadcasted at 10 p.m. November 10, 1938. It is stated upon authority believed to be reliable, that most of the evening was employed in drawing up lists of fated victims. Several persons known to this office were aware at 9 p.m. on the evening of November 9th, 1938, that the 'spontaneous' outrage was scheduled for that night sometime after midnight and several of such persons interviewed, stayed up purposely in order to witness it.

At 3 a.m. November 10, 1938, was unleashed a barrage of Nazi ferocity as had had no equal hitherto in Germany, or very likely anywhere else in the world since savagery, if ever. Jewish dwellings were smashed into and contents demolished or looted. In one of the Jewish sections an eighteen year old boy was hurled from a three story window to land with both legs broken on a street littered with burning beds and other household furniture and effects from his family's and other apartments. This information was supplied by an attending physician. It is reported from another quarter that among domestic effects thrown out of a Jewish dwelling, a small dog descended four flights to a broken spine on a cluttered street. Although apparently centred in poor districts, the raid was not confined to the humble classes. One apartment of exceptionally refined occupants known to this office, was violently ransacked, presumably in a search for valuables that was not in vain, and one of the marauders thrust a cane through a priceless medieval painting portraying a biblical scene. Another apartment of the same category is known to have been turned upside down in the frenzied course of whatever the invaders were after. Reported loss of looting of cash, silver, jewellery, and otherwise easily convertible articles, have been frequent.

Jewish shop windows by the hundreds were systematically and wantonly smashed throughout the entire city at a loss estimated at several millions of marks. There are reports that substantial losses have been sustained on the famous Leipzig 'Bruhl', as many of the shop windows at the time of the demolition were filled with costly furs that were seized before the windows could be boarded up. In proportion to the general destruction of real estate, however, losses of goods are felt to have been relatively small. The spectators who viewed the wreckage when daylight had arrived were mostly in such a bewildered mood, that there was no danger of impulsive acts, and the perpetrators probably were too busy in carrying out their schedule to take off a whole lot of time for personal profit. At all events, the main streets of the city were a positive litter of shattered plate glass. According to reliable testimony, the debacle was executed by S. S. men and Storm Troopers not in uniform, each group having been provided with hammers, axes, crowbars and incendiary bombs.

Three synagogues in Leipzig were fired simultaneously by incendiary bombs and all sacred objects and records desecrated or destroyed, in most instances hurled through the windows and burned in the streets. No attempts whatsoever were made to quench the fires, functions of the fire brigade having been con-confined to playing water on adjoining buildings. All of the synagogues were irreparably gutted by flames, and the walls of the two that are in the close proximity of the consulate are now being razed. The blackened frames have been centres of attraction during the past week of terror for eloquently silent and bewildered crowds. One of the largest clothing stores in the heart of the city was destroyed by flames from incendiary bombs, only the charred walls and gutted roof having been left standing. As was the case with the synagogues, no attempts on the part of the fire brigade were made to extinguish the fire, although apparently there was a certain amount of apprehension for adjacent property, for the walls of a coffee house next door were covered with asbestos and sprayed by the doughty firemen. It is extremely difficult to believe, but the owners of the clothing store were actually charged with setting the fire and on that basis were dragged from their beds at 6 a.m. and clapped into prison.

Tactics which closely approached the ghoulish took place at the Jewish cemetery where the temple was fired together with a building occupied by caretakers, tombstones uprooted and graves violated. Eye-witnesses considered reliable report that ten corpses were left unburied at this cemetery for a week's time because all grave diggers and cemetery attendants had been arrested.

Ferocious as was the violation of property, the most hideous phase of the so-called 'spontaneous' action, has been the wholesale arrest and transportation to concentration camps of male German Jews between the ages of sixteen and sixty, as well as Jewish men without citizenship. This has been taking place daily since the night of horror. This office has no way of accurately checking the numbers of such arrests, but there is very little question that they have gone into several thousands in Leipzig alone. Having demolished dwellings and hurled most of the moveable effects to the streets, the insatiably sadistic perpetrators threw many of the trembling inmates into a small stream that flows through the Zoological Park, commanding horrified spectators to spit at them, defile them with mud and jeer at their plight. The latter incident has been repeatedly corroborated by German witnesses who were nauseated in telling the tale. The slightest manifestation of sympathy evoked a positive fury on the part of the perpetrators, and the crowd was powerless to do anything but turn horror-stricken eyes from the scene of abuse, or leave the vicinity. These tactics were carried out the entire morning of November 10th without police intervention and they were applied to men, women and children.

There is much evidence of physical violence, including several deaths. At least half a dozen cases have been personally observed, victims with bloody, badly bruised faces having fled to this office, believing that as refugees their desire to emigrate could be expedited here. As a matter of fact this consulate has been a bedlam of humanity for the past ten days, most of these visitors being desperate women, as their husbands and sons had been taken off to concentration camps.[13]

The confidential report which the American Consul in Stuttgart sent to his ambassador is no less staggering than the reports of his colleagues in north and central Germany. 'I have the honour to report,' Samuel W. Honaker wrote, 'that the Jews of south-west Germany have suffered vicissitudes during the last three days which would seem unreal to one living in an enlightened country during the twentieth century if one had not actually been a witness of their dreadful experiences, or if one had not had them corroborated by more than one person of undoubted integrity.'[14]

Once again, Bavaria distinguished itself for the violence with which Jews were persecuted within its boundaries. Arrests began at three in the morning of November 10th in Munich,[15] where the main synagogue had been destroyed in the summer of 1938. When the police hammered at the door of Emil Kraemer, a partner in the Aufhäuser Bank, which for many generations had managed the fortune of the Bavarian royal family, he and his wife threw themselves from a third-floor window of their building. Six thousand Jews were arrested on that day and taken to Dachau, while a Protestant minister in the city spoke in his sermon on the theme of 'God's will be done,' from St Matthew, saying that it was written in the Scriptures that the blood of Christ would be visited upon the Jews. Although no date had been specified in the prophecy, the hour seemed to have struck and the Jews' fates to have been ordained by divine will.

The SA and the SS behaved with particular savagery in Nuremberg,[16] where the main synagogue had already been demolished a few months before on the orders of the District Party Leader, Streicher. From dawn on November 10th, apartments were rifled and their inhabitants molested. (Jewish shops in this antisemitic hell had already been plundered before.) One victim, who was attacked with a dagger and tried to cover his head with his hands, had two of his fingers shattered. His wife, who rushed to his defence, was hit on the head and pushed down the stairs. Jacob Spaeth was beaten to death. Simon Loeb, who lived at 22 Pirkheimerstrasse, was found dead at home. Paul Lebrecht, who was thrown by the Nazis into a courtyard, was left dangling from the railings of a balcony, where he was found dead. Herr Bamberger suffered a heart attack while his flat was being wrecked. Paul Astruck was dragged from his bed and taken to a wood, where his body was later found, horribly mutilated. Nathan Langstadt was found in his bath at 47 Ranke-strasse with his throat cut. The secretary of the Jewish congregation in Nuremberg counted nine murders on November 10th alone, as well as ten suicides, half of them women.

In the neighbouring city of Fürth also, sadism was unrestrained. All of the Jews, including infants, sick people and pregnant women, were roused from their beds between two and half-past two in the morning. They were first taken to a theatre, where some were made to sit in the dark while others were beaten under blinding spot-lights on the stage. They were afterwards herded into the market square, most of them half-dressed, and were kept on their feet until five in the morning. Women, children and the ill were then sent home while the men, ruthlessly manhandled, were taken to the camp at Dachau.

In the village of Lichtenfels in Upper Franconia, a Jewish woman, who tried to save the sacred objects from fire, was murdered by children who then played catch with the prayer books. The Jews were driven out of the Bavarian town of Ingolstadt and made to walk to Munich.

Synagogues were burned in all the southern cities – Freiburg, Karlsruhe, Heidelberg, Heilbronn, Tübingen – even in small villages. Flames were reflected on the rooftops of Stuttgart, the capital of Württemberg, at three in the morning. The scene was described by *The National Socialist Courier* under the headline 'Just Vengeance by Outraged Citizens'. 'The midnight spectacle,' the newspaper reported 'drew an appropriately sizeable number of spectators. All of them appeared satisfied that the crimes of the Jews were being avenged, even if only in limited measure. Impressive discipline was exercised throughout the operation.' The main street, Königstrasse, was so choked with onlookers that traffic had to be re-routed. The streets were strewn with glass and SS patrols, acting as law officers, kept watch over the wrecked shops while their proprietors boarded up the gaping windows.

Celebration was not as widespread, however, as the *National Socialist Courier* claimed. One of its journalists deplored the 'soft-hearted squeamishness' of some of the spectators in an article of November 12th–13th entitled 'Dialogue with Our Readers': 'Swabians are reputed to be sentimental, but this does not mean that they are delicate. . . . I have heard a few people whimpering and complaining about operations against the Jews in the past few days. They decry a few Jewish speculators' broken windows and mourn the loss of synagogues. . . . The more devious allude to a "bolshevik situation" and the absence of culture and authority. We can scarcely believe that in 1938 there is still anyone so blind. How many of them, especially the women, still buy goods from Jewish shops? Let no one argue that they are cheaper. . . . Such simpletons are beneath contempt.' The article concluded with the exhortation : 'Be thankful to live in such glorious times. Who would have thought that our generation would attain such momentous accomplishments? Posterity will envy our good fortune.'

And glorious the accomplishments were. Setting aside the devastation of Jewish homes in Stuttgart, the city could boast the suicide of twenty-nine-year-old teacher Felix David, of his twenty-seven-year-old wife Ruth, and the deaths of their two babies, Benjamin (two) and Gideon (born in 1938).

A number of priests were among the 'delicate' souls deplored by the *National Socialist Courier*. In the tiny parish of Oberlennigen in Württemberg, Pastor Julius van Jan denounced the pogrom from his pulpit.

Today the German people must ask themselves where in Germany is the prophet sent to proclaim God's word in the house of the king. Where is the man who in the name of God and of justice will repeat the words of Jeremiah (22 :2–9): 'Execute ye judgment and righteousness, and deliver the spoiled out of the hand of the oppressor: and do no wrong, do no violence to the stranger, the fatherless, nor the widow, neither shed innocent blood in this place.' God has sent us such men but they are all either in concentration camps or condemned to silence. Those who enter the houses of kings to worship propagate falsehoods no less than the nationalistic zealots in the time of Jeremiah. They can only shout 'Heil!' and 'Victory!' without preaching God's word. . . .

Recommending contrition and remorse, Julius van Jan continued:

Who would have believed that the murder of one man in Paris could lead to so many murders here in Germany? . . . Passions run riot and the divine commandments are mocked. Places of worship, which some would regard as holy places, have been burnt without restraint and the stranger's possessions have been plundered and destroyed. Men who have loyally served the German people have been thrown into concentration camps simply because they belong to another race. . . . God may uplift a man or a people to the loftiest honours, but if they close their hearts to God's word they will suddenly be cast into the abyss.[17]

This sermon cost the courageous pastor a term of imprisonment and internment in a concentration camp.

A young man named Krugel, who was a theology student at the University of Tübingen, submitted his resignation from the 180th SA company, declaring in his letter to the commander:[18] 'I regard the Jews as our people's most treacherous enemies at the present time. Any legal measure taken to oppose them would be completely justified. But illegal measures could easily have been prevented by the Party and its organizations. The licence granted is a vindication of "mob rage", which is now justified in settling any debate. As a Christian I cannot share this concept of justice and I can no longer accept before my conscience and before the Christian community my continued membership of the SA.'

The Lutheran Bishop of Württemberg resisted the pressure of 170 priests and militants in the Kirchlich Teologische Sozietät to authorize an official denunciation of the 'Crystal Night' from Lutheran pulpits. Like the majority of Catholic and Protestant clergy, the bishop's first concern was to preserve his own ecclesiastical institutions. A courageous man, he sent several letters to high-ranking government officials denouncing euthanasia and the extermination of the Jews. But, two weeks after the pogrom, when he protested to the Minister of Justice he unwittingly expressed the deeply nationalist and antisemitic sentiments with which German Christianity was imbued at this time.

'I do not contest the right of the state to thwart the menace of Judaism. Since my youth I have recognized the truth in the statements by Heinrich von Treitschke[19] and Adolf Stoecker[20] concerning the corrosive influence which Judaism exerts in religious, moral, cultural, economic and political spheres.'

If Hitler intended to judge the Jews, the bishop continued, he should bear in mind that those who judged in God's name must answer to God. Transgression against God's commandments would eventually be punished. Stressing his continued loyalty to the National Socialist government, Bishop Wurm concluded, 'I have advised the pastors of our bishopric to avoid any gesture which, given the charged atmosphere at present, could be interpreted as provocation, but I have added that they must allow no expression of grief or commiseration with the Jews to be construed as treason towards the state.'[21]

For all its lapses of logic, the bishop's protest was a courageous gesture amid – as the Reverend Wilhelm Niemoeller[22] remarked on the eve of the war – the stifling silence of the German people.

Near Württemberg, the pogrom at the international health resort of Baden-Baden was deferred until seven in the morning so as not to disturb the sleep of the late-season visitors. Baden-Baden had previously been relatively peaceful, because its foreign visitors and the foreign currency which they spent were badly needed by the Reich. The Jews were arrested under the supervision of policemen in resplendent uniforms. They were taken to the prison courtyard and kept there until midday. Dr Arthur Flehinger, a retired teacher at the Baden-Baden gymnasium, relates:

Towards noon the main gates were opened and our group, disarmed and arrayed in orderly ranks by the guards, was marched across town behind a Star of David over which had been written, 'God, do not abandon us'.

They had waited until there were large numbers of people in the streets, so as to give them a show, but most of the inhabitants of Baden-Baden creditably kept out of sight.

The spectators who did turn out were of the basest kind. Three teachers behaved particularly badly, promising treats to their young pupils to encourage them to shout 'Death to Judas' as we passed. I saw people sobbing behind their curtains. I even heard one of them say, 'I did not see Christ; I saw a whole rank of Christs march past with their heads high, not bent under a burden of guilt.' Photographs of the parade were taken and are now on display in the synagogue built by the French occupying forces after the war.

The parade reached the synagogue, whose top steps were already lined with people in uniform and in civilian clothing. Passing in front of them, we had to endure their petty insults. For the whole of the march I had looked people straight in the eye, and as we reached the top of the steps a man shouted, 'Wipe that insolent expression off your face, Professor.' It was a confession of weakness and fear rather than an insult. Later at Dachau I discovered that the 'Nazi masters' could not endure a hard look.

At this moment Dr Hauser, an eminent lawyer who later died with his wife at Auschwitz, was seized and shoved on to a prayer shawl which the Nazis had thrown down for us to walk over.

The interior of the synagogue had changed completely. It was swarming with SS troops. There were large numbers of them in the women's gallery, where they were laying electric cables. They were not from Baden-Baden. They had been called in from the surrounding towns to ensure that personal feelings would not interfere with what they had to do.

Suddenly a thick, arrogant voice commanded, 'You will all sing the *Horst Wessel Lied*.' We were forced to sing it twice. Then I was summoned to the dais to read a passage from *Mein Kampf*. I began softly, but the SS trooper behind me grew irritated and struck me on the back of my neck. Those who read afterwards received the same treatment.

During a lull we all had to troop out into the courtyard to relieve ourselves. We were not permitted to use the WC; we had to face the synagogue while being kicked from behind.

We were taken from the synagogue to the Central Hotel opposite; the owner had to produce a meal for 70 people without warning.

Everyone wondered what would happen to us. We had been closed off from the world without knowing what to expect. Then the minister, ashen-faced, came into the dining-room. 'Our synagogue is on fire.' We understood now why the electric cables had been laid. One of the more callous guards remarked, 'If it had been up to me you would all have been blown up with the synagogue.'

A bus was waiting outside the door, surrounded by an impressive flock of 'outraged citizens'. We ran to the bus, and those who did not run fast enough were beaten. At the station a special train arrived from Freiburg to collect the Jews from our area. A policeman, silent as a tomb, stood watch over each compartment. After Karlsruhe, when the train branched off in the direction of Stuttgart, the only word to be heard was the terrible name Dachau.[23]

In Frankfurt the Jewish population numbered 35,000; there were three synagogues, the famous Philantropin Institute for advanced studies founded in 1805, and many Jewish and social and cultural organizations, including a museum sponsored by the Rothschild family. Hundreds of terrified Jews streamed into the office of the British Consul, Smallbones, who ignored the order not to intervene and did all he could to help them. Smallbones was in constant touch with Captain Foley in Berlin, to obtain emigration permits for England and Palestine. He was able to help Professor Martin Buber.

For several days the basement of the consulate provided a shelter and food to Jews hunted by the Gestapo.

According to his report and reports by other witnesses,[24] the pogrom in Frankfurt began with a fire in the synagogue at five in the morning of November 10th. Young Jews were forced to cut up the scrolls of the Law (Tora) and to burn them. Some superstitious Nazis even pocketed a few scraps of the scrolls for good luck.

At about half-past six most Jewish homes were invaded by squads of between five and ten men. At 6.45 two SS troopers knocked at the door of Julius Meyer, a lawyer and one of the directors of the Jewish congregation. They behaved very 'correctly'.

'Were you expecting us? You must have heard the news.'

'Yes, I expected you. We are not blind. We saw what was going on.'

'Do not feel that we would be inhuman if we carried out a search. It is our duty.'

'Please, gentlemen. I understand that you are carrying out orders.'

Julius Meyer recalled at that moment having carried out similar orders during the First World War.

One of the Gestapo agents called him into a room next door, so as to avoid any accusation of maltreating Frau Meyer, who opened the cupboards for him. Despite the circumstances, he praised her for her good house-keeping and chatted to Julius Meyer as he handed over his 'arms' – a dagger which he had brought back from the First World War and the rifle issued to him on active service.

'I'll give you my sword.'

'From active service !'

A private car was waiting outside to take Dr Meyer to the assembly point, the festival hall where he had many times heard the chorus sing 'All men shall be brothers' from Beethoven's Ninth Symphony. A Gestapo agent snatched from him the decorations which he was carrying.

'You got them on the home front.'

Meyer was asked what his occupation was.

'Lawyer.'

'Another shyster.'

'I am a court counsellor.'

'There is no law any more.'

'There is German law.'

The man gave a feeble smile. 'Come on. Let's go.'

SS troopers lined them up to do exercises to keep them warm. 'Stretch, bend, bend, kneel.' A man slumped down dead from exhaustion. The rest had to shout, 'We are Jews.' Then they had to sing an old marching song. Finally they were allowed to go down to the wash-basins to moisten their parched throats, like cattle.

Upstairs the SS were dragging an old man by his beard. He was wearing a prayer shawl (Talit) and carrying the scrolls (Tefillin). They wanted to parade him before their comrades. The crowd began shouting, 'Pray, old man, pray!' The old man stood petrified. One of the Jews put the prayer shawl on himself and began to recite the 'Schema Israel' in a sharp clear voice.

'Hear, O Israel. The Lord is our God, the Lord is one.'

All the Jews chanted with him in unison. The astounded SS troopers ordered them to stop.

Then an SA trooper, who had taken Rabbi Salzberger to fetch his prayer shawl from the rubbish bins, brought him into the room and ordered him to recite the Ten Commandments.

Some other SA men turned his hat back to front and took his photograph with great hilarity. Then they ordered him to shout a hundred times, 'O, Lord, give us Moses, for we are of his religion.' And after this they sang the 'Song of the Red Sea': 'If the Jews had drowned as they tried to cross, there would now be peace on earth.'

A high-ranking Nazi officer arrived and the rabbi was presented to him.

'How old are you?'

'Fifty-six.'

'You are well preserved, but why do you not have a beard?'

'I am a reform rabbi.'

'Do you have such things?'

Their conversation was interrupted by a voice from the balcony

The SS Obergruppenführer had ordered a Jewish opera singer to perform the famous aria from *The Magic Flute*, 'In this sacred grove which knows no hate'. There was much laughter, and more still when the photographer took pictures of some of the others. It was not clear what purpose they would serve.

After a day without food they were brought bread and sausages with a little tea before boarding a special train. They were then taken to Buchenwald.

In the Rhineland, where vom Rath's funeral was to be held, the pogrom was unrestrained. Rabbi Eschelbacher of Düsseldorf[25] had returned with his wife from an evening with friends to receive a terrified call at 11.45 from one Frau Blumenthal, who lived near the Jewish congregation buildings. 'Doctor Eschelbacher,' she said, 'They are tearing down the community house and beating people up. I can hear them screaming from here.'

Just as the rabbi was about to set out for the community house, someone pounded at his door. He switched off his lights and peered into the square before his house, which was swarming with SA troopers. A moment later the SA reached the top of the stairs. Smashing through his door, they plunged into his flat shouting, 'Vengeance for Paris. Down with the Jews.' They brought out wooden mallets from their bags and began breaking the furniture, shattering the glass panels of the cupboards and the windows. Then they fell on Dr Eschelbacher. One of them grabbed him and ordered him downstairs. Thinking that he was about to die, the rabbi asked to go to his bedroom where he left his watch, his wallet and his keys and bade farewell to his wife. 'Chazak!' she said. 'Be brave.'

The rabbi found himself at the foot of the stairs without knowing how he got there. Outside there were fifty or sixty SA troopers shouting, 'Here. Try preaching now!' Dr Eschelbacher began talking about Counsellor vom Rath's murder: it was worse for the Jews than for the Germans and his fellow Jews were not to blame. A weird debate ensued. One of the SA men said to him, 'You remember your fiery speech at the concert hall when you talked about religion and antisemitism?'

Another, wielding the leg of a chair, threatened the rabbi's skull, but a third held him back. 'At the GPU you would have had a bullet in the back of the neck a long time ago.'

The street corner was scattered with books, files, and letters flung from the rabbi's windows. His typewriter landed on the pile. An SA man grabbed Dr Eschelbacher and pushed him against the wall of the house opposite. Then he was shut into a hall closet where the local Party official arrested him 'to ensure his protection' and to escort him to police headquarters. Flanked by SA men, Rabbi Eschelbacher and his neighbours, the Wertheimers, were taken to the police station, Frau Wertheimer in her pyjamas, while bystanders jeered at them.

Others unluckily did not escape the uncontrolled mob. Paul Marcus, owner of the Karena café-restaurant, was shot trying to escape after his establishment had been wrecked. At the near-by village of Hilden a mother and her son, Carl Herz, and Nathan Meyer were all stabbed to death with pitchforks. Also at Hilden, Dr Sommer, an assimilated Jew married to a gentile, poisoned himself with his wife and their aged servant at the end of their garden. Their bodies were delivered up by the Gestapo in leaden coffins and no Jew, apart from the reader, Rosenbusch, who recited prayers, was permitted to attend their funerals. No legal inquiry was ever undertaken.

Two seventy-year-old Jews were killed on the same night at Düsseldorf, while many others were gravely injured. The wife of the restaurant owner who had been shot was riddled with several bullets, including one in the abdomen, and was confined secretly in Düsseldorf hospital, while the Gestapo tried to extract from her a declaration that her husband had committed suicide. In isolation rooms the same hospital cared for Oscar Koch, who had received six wounds, his hands heavily suppurating beneath his bandages, and Simon Eimer, who had jumped from a window on the night of the massacre and shattered his pelvis and both legs. Dr Oppenheimer's wife suffered a serious head injury and was admitted to St Mary's Catholic Hospital. In the same room with her was the aged Frau

Gabriel, who, despite her seventy years, had also leapt from her window. On the night of the pogrom the Catholic hospital swarmed with Jews in need of first-aid. A chemist, Dr Schneider, was found unconscious in the street. Dr Lehmann was struck on the head and suffered concussion. The Kleins were massively bruised after being rolled step by step from the third floor of their building. Rudolf Weil, who had only recently settled in Düsseldorf, had been savagely beaten about the head and left for dead on the pavement; he died, probably of shock, a few weeks later.

Aged Gustav Oppenheim and his wife were so badly battered that they had to be admitted to a convalescent home. The SA had chased their daughter-in-law, shouting, 'Where is the old man's whore?' When they found Frau Cohn in her bedroom, they pulled her from her bed, ripped her nightdress and beat her livid until an angry SS trooper yanked her away to the stairs, muttering, 'Come with me. I can't stomach any more of this.' He dragged her to the foot of the stairs and struck her a blow that sent her hurtling into the street on top of her mother-in-law, who lay unconscious on the doorstep. She was taken barefoot in her tattered, blood-stained nightdress to the police station, where a police officer found an apron for her to wear.

Judge Efraim, who was left with a broken jaw and unable to walk, was forced to eat baby foods for many weeks. Along the streets of the town, the homes and shops of Jews presented a grisly spectacle. The SA troopers poured hydrochloric acid on the work-benches of tailor Albert Wolf and broke his work tools. They even tossed the plates and pots and pans of some of the poorer people out of their windows. Valuable equipment in the consulting-rooms of Jewish doctors was wrecked. Dr Loewenberg's up-to-date radiography equipment was destroyed. Dr Otto, burgomaster of Düsseldorf, was said to have supervised personally the demolition of Steinberg's dress shop. In fact, all the civic dignitaries joined in the pogrom. (This was not the case in other towns, except Wurtzburg, where the rector of the university was prompt to lend a helping hand to the 'avengers'.)

In Düsseldorf, doctors from the hospital and a number of judges helped to set fire to the main synagogue. A near-by chemist supplied petrol while some squads found some pitch. The scrolls were removed from the Ark and flung into the fire while some of the arsonists danced round it in the robes of the rabbi and the cantors.

The rabbi of this congregation, one of the most brilliant in Germany, was searched by the police, who confiscated all he had on him.

'Let me keep my braces, please. I assure you that I shall not try to hang myself.'

'That's a pity,' one of them replied.

'You want to live,' another jeered, 'but you Jews have nothing to live or die for.'

'You haven't the slightest notion what a Jew is,' Dr Eschelbacher answered gravely.

His wife arrived, bringing underwear and toilet articles. 'Chazak!' ('Be brave!') she murmered again before she left.

The night dragged on for the rabbi, locked in his cell. At about two o'clock in the morning the lights were suddenly switched on. A police major and another officer stalked into his cell to ask whether there was another synagogue in Düsseldorf besides the one in the street by the barracks. Dr Eschelbacher replied that there was not. He was left alone until six, when it was time to wash. He was not allowed to exchange a word with the other members of the congregation whom he saw.

Dr Eschelbacher was locked in a cell with three non-practising Jews for the next three days. When he chanted afternoon prayers (Minha), the others watched silently with their hats on in accordance with Jewish law. Together they recited the prayer of the dead. The rabbi explained the psalms and taught them the song of Juda Halevy, 'Jaawer olai rezonokh,' which they found deeply moving. Afterwards they defied the prison gloom by performing gymnastics within the narrow confines of their cell. But their conversation soon revolved around their worries about what lay in store for them. Two of the non-practising Jews, Berger and Lesser, were nagged by an additional worry: their wives were not Jewish. Apart from their collective anxieties, the turn of events placed the survival of their marriages in jeopardy (especially Lesser, whose wife had insisted that their son be given a Catholic education). Neither man was confident that marital devotion would prevail over deep-rooted prejudice.

The practical arrangements of the prison also created problems. For the four Jews, all together in a small cell with only three mattresses between them, the nights seemed interminable. Crammed one against another without being able to turn over, shivering from the lack of sufficient covers, they waited for dawn to recover from the night. In the morning they were given only three minutes to wash and to see the other prisoners and had to run to the washbasins. Their diet consisted fundamentally of water, disguised as ersatz coffee, potato or split-pea soup, garnished with a sliver of bread, or rice pudding in the evening. Their drinking water was kept in a tin jug to avoid suicides and was tepid. Their guards, unaccustomed to coping with so many prisoners, were jumpy and exasperated.

Dr Eschelbacher's prison conditions altered completely after three days. For no apparent reason he was moved to a private cell and given books to read, one of which, by a curious chance, was the novel *Siebenkäs* by Jean Paul (Richter). The principal theme of the novel is the same as that of a Yom Kippur sermon in which he had tried to encourage the anguish stricken faithful. The sermon dwells on Adam on the first night after his expulsion, when at sunset he complained, 'Woe is me, the earth darkens and returns to chaos because I have sinned.' Adam wept all night, and Eve, seated beside him, also wept. But when the sun rose they understood that this was the order of the world and they offered a sacrifice to the Creator. The novelist compares Adam's sensation with that of his hero when he realized that his family was breaking up. 'He felt as Adam when he feared that the first night outside Paradise was the end of the world, and understood the next morning that it was the way of the world.'

This mingling of the Talmudic and German literatures gave the rabbi fresh hope and faith during the pogrom. Isolated in his cell, he spent hours thinking of God and man and Judaism and his own fate. In the next cell was Dr Franke, who had been a lecturer on modern and contemporary history at the Institute of Political Science in Berlin and general secretary of the Association of Catholic Students of Germany. Now in his second year in custody, he had earned the privilege of receiving newspapers. Thanks to him, the rabbi was able to learn what was happening in the Reich.

Another unexpected comfort was proffered by a guard who produced from his pocket an object wrapped in white paper and handed it to the rabbi, respectfully explaining that 'the fifty-two other Jewish inmates locked up together in the basement sent this with their greetings'.

Dr Eschelbacher found that it contained a sausage. He thanked the guard but asked him to take it back as he would be unable to eat it.

'The others eat it.'

'I respect the dietary laws (Kosher), but every Jew must obey his conscience.'

'No one will see you,' the guard replied, 'and it will be good for you.'

'Yes, but God is watching,' the rabbi said.

The astonished guard repeated the story throughout the prison.

Not satisfied with burning down synagogues, plundering Jewish shops and homes, and terrorizing their occupants, the Nazis invaded Jewish hospitals, old people's homes, and children's homes. Dr Herz, who later fled to Australia and was awarded a prize from Harvard University in 1940 for his book *Life in Germany*, described the days in November 1938 when he was temporarily director of a Rhineland orphanage at Dinslaken. At about 5.45 in the morning of November 10th he was awakened by a vigorous ringing of the door-bell. Throwing a coat over his shoulders, he went to answer. Two Gestapo officers and a policeman announced that they had come to search for arms, as they were searching all Jewish homes. They cut the telephone wires, rummaged through drawers and books and searched for money. The orphanage ordinarily held its religious services at seven o'clock. While the three officers continued the search, the staff and the children, forty-six persons in all, of whom thirty-two were orphans between six and sixteen years old, recited their prayers with no inkling of what was happening. Then Dr Herz called them to the refectory to tell them. 'Be brave,' he said, 'have faith in God. We'll get over these difficult times.'

After eating breakfast together, they went off to their separate tasks until 9.30, when the door-bell was violently rung. As soon as the door was unlatched, fifty men burst into the building. They stormed into the refectory, which luckily was empty, and began systematically wrecking the place. The children screamed with terror. Flouting a Gestapo order, Dr Herz told them to follow him into the street. He thought that the troopers would not dare harm the children out in the open. Despite the cold and wet, the children scrambled into the street, bareheaded and without coats, running after the director down to the town hall to obtain the protection of the police.

There were about ten policemen and a crowd of onlookers eager for excitement.

'We do not give protection to Jews,' the police sergeant said. 'Get out with those children or I'll shoot.'

'All right. Kill me and the children. That way the matter will be settled.'

The policeman gave a cynical smile, aimed his gun at the gate that led to the orphanage garden, and fired, shattering the lock. He forced the group on to the wet grass in front of the orphanage building, ordering them not to leave for any reason.

Sirens began whining at 10.15. A thick cloud of smoke drifted up from the neighbourhood of the synagogue. Smaller trails of smoke pinpointed houses on fire.

At 10.45 the Dinslaken police chief arrived to 'study the situation' with Dr Herz. 'What do you intend doing?' he asked.

'I want permission from the authorities straight away to take these children to Belgium or Holland.'

While two men strolled through the orphanage, picking their way among heaps of rubble that had been left, a young man in civilian clothes asked the police chief in a sharp voice, 'What does this Jew want of you?'

The chief was probably frightened and shouted at Dr Herz, 'Hurry up and join the other Jews.'

Policemen came and led him to the school near the synagogue where forty Jews from the town had been assembled. The commanding officer ordered Dr Herz to take charge of the others who had been arrested and act as their spokesman, making a list of their names. A former director of a business school, who had previously been a city councillor at Dinslaken, sat groaning and holding his head, which was streaming with blood. From a near-by tap, Dr Herz managed to collect some water for him in an envelope.

The local Nazi Party leader appeared, in civilian clothes. 'Unknown persons are responsible for the destruction which occurred this morning,' he announced. 'Their reasons can easily be understood. A mother and father in Düsseldorf are mourning their son who was murdered in the flower of his youth by a Jew. It is understandable. No one will lay a finger on you. You have nothing to be afraid of. After all, we are not in Russia. . . . The doctor will soon be here. If you are hungry, collect your money – you will certainly have enough – and one of you may go and buy some food.'

He paused and then added, 'The cow which belonged to the orphanage has been given to a German peasant who will feed it. Animals must not be made to suffer for what happens.'

At half-past six in the evening the Party leader returned, this time in uniform. He told the group to assemble in a room at an hotel in the town centre. The children were shuffled into a cart and the adults followed on foot.

The cart crawled to the hotel through a mob of curious onlookers. The hotel ballroom had been strewn with straw, and pillows had been taken from the orphanage. A curtain had been draped over a portrait of Hitler on the stage before the Jews arrived. They were served stew, with the SA commander's assurance that it contained nothing harmful. At about eight o'clock men over sixteen years old trooped off to sleep in a stable. The curfew began at ten, but it was impossible to get the children to settle down in the normal way with forty uniformed SS and SA troopers standing by. Summoning up his courage, Dr Herz decided to act with the children as though nothing were wrong. He began chanting evening prayers in a sharp clear voice. The children recited with him. The speechless Nazis withdrew, leaving only a police officer and a single SA trooper to stand guard.

The following morning, an official from the town hall arrived to purchase food with the 132 marks found at the orphanage. The orphanage staff were allowed to prepare the meal. While they were alone with the prisoners, the policemen explained that they had had nothing to do with the events of the previous evening. 'They got us out of bed at four in the morning with orders to report to the town hall. The police were supposed not to intervene until four o'clock in the afternoon. We were to allow the Party to do as it liked until then. Apart from the commander, we are all good Social Democrats or Democrats, but what can we do in times like these?'

That afternoon the police chief's assistant asked Dr Herz to return to the orphanage with him to hand over all the keys to the regional commander of the Party. Dr Herz was led to the refectory before about forty SA troopers. The regional commander, a former teacher, snatched the keys from his hand and ordered him into the courtyard. From the window he shouted, 'Come here, criminal; it seems you've been complaining about being maltreated.'

'There must be some mistake.'

'A policeman told me. Officers do not lie.'

'The officer was mistaken.'

'You wait here, you criminal, until I call you.'

Some young people in civilian clothes were carrying off the objects which had not been destroyed, mostly books from the library.

'What do you want, Jew?' one of them shouted.

'I'm waiting for the regional commander.'

'Commander,' one of them shouted to the regional commander, who was talking with the police chief. 'There's a Jew waiting for you here.'

'Tell him to get lost.'

That evening relatives of the children, anxious at having received no news from them, telephoned from Anvers, Brussels and Amsterdam. On November 15th the police took the director and the children back to the remains of the orphanage because the hotel owners needed the ballroom for a boxing match. The Party leaders forbade local tradesmen to make any deliveries or render any services to the orphanage. The children were forced to load the few possessions still remaining to them on to a carriage which took them to Cologne. Here the Jewish community – or the vestiges of it – took them into their care.

The NSDAP used the orphanage funds to build a new regional headquarters for the Party. The story of the Dinslaken orphanage ends here. The children were allowed to go to Belgium and Holland in January 1939, but it is not known whether or not their persecutors finally caught up with them a few months later.

4

The Quarry

It was Dr Goebbels, impresario of the pogrom, who issued the order to end it, and his order was released in the Berlin press at five o'clock in the evening of November 10th. By eight o'clock all the radio stations in Germany were sending out his appeal to staunch the 'spontaneous phase' of action against the Jews :

> The natural and fully justified outrage felt by the German people at the brutal Jewish assassination in Paris has been expressed this evening in reprisals against Jewish shops and businesses.
>
> I now appeal to the entire population to desist at once from any further demonstrations or action against the Jews. The last word on the Paris assassination will be spoken in legislation.

The Reich security services also broadcast to all police forces instructions to restore order. Reinhard Heydrich dispatched cable after cable from his Berlin headquarters.[1]

> Further to my previous instructions, I repeat that any act of plunder committed in the course of protest demonstrations must be firmly suppressed by the immediate apprehension and arrest of those responsible, and by the recovery of stolen property. As previously stated in the press and on the radio, protest demonstrations must cease. The law-enforcement agencies will co-

ordinate to reinforce patrols tonight. Any further demonstrations must be prevented, as far as possible, bearing in mind the legitimate indignation of the population. Pillaging must be dealt with severely.

Here the security chief groped for a way of condemning the same 'comrades' to whom he had previously given a free hand. He needed to find the words to explain that 'amateurs' must now yield to 'professionals'.

'It may be necessary,' Heydrich allowed, 'to call upon the crime squad to carry out investigations, but further instructions must be sought before any cases are passed on to an examining magistrate.'

'Every effort,' he continued, 'must be made to halt pillaging. Pillagers must be detained by the Police.'

As to what to do with them, he emphasized, 'The Minister of Justice has indicated that formal arrest warrants need not be issued against persons taken into custody during demonstrations. He requests that the Reich prosecutors not keep files of cases arising from action against Jews.'

Uniformed police patrols, which had been spirited away, suddenly materialized on every street corner. They were unsuccessful, however, in preventing further incidents. Each local Party group yearned for the glory of having organized its own pogrom, of winning a place for itself in the roll of honour of the 'Crystal Night'. Reports streamed in from SS and SA brigade commanders throughout Germany, each jostling for first place as a burner of synagogues, or ransacker of Jewish homes and shops. The Fiftieth SA Brigade at Darmstadt proudly boasted of having burned down and dynamited thirty-seven synagogues within its sector.[2]

Damage was especially severe in Berlin. The jeweller Margraf alone, in the famous street Unter Den Linden, sustained losses amounting to 1,700,000 marks. Even the branch offices of such French companies as Citroën or Etam, the manufacturer of women's underwear, were wrecked. Those Jews who escaped arrest were made to shovel up the broken glass from the pavements and plank over their gaping shopfronts. Notices offering shops for rent, or announcing 'Shop sold to Aryans', appeared more or less everywhere. To foreign journalists who were shocked by the scope and the ferocity of the demonstrations, Goebbels cynically retorted, 'Imagine the outcome if we had organized it.'[3]

While the Minister of Propaganda handed out startling pronouncements, Marshal Goering, mastermind of the Four Year Plan, was eager to clear away the debris. At his request Reinhard Heydrich drew up a balance sheet of the pogrom. The cost turned out to be heavy. Although the razing of 267 synagogues and congregation buildings may not have cut into the German economy, the damage to movable and immovable property certainly did – and not least the damage to 7,500 Jewish shops, the entire number which still remained in the Reich before the pogrom. Goering and his colleagues who were responsible for the economy worried about the growing frequency with which the Nazi barons authorized plunder for the benefit of their local fiefs without showing much concern for the needs of the State.

In Bavaria, of which Streicher was District Party Leader, illegal confiscation and corruption were so widespread that Goering appointed a special commission of inquiry to prepare a confidential report.[4]

'I regarded the events of the night of November 9th and the following day,' Deputy District Party Leader Holz testified before the commission, 'as a sign that the Jewish question would be treated in a new way throughout the Reich. Jewish schools and synagogues were burnt and property in Jewish homes and shops was destroyed. The police also sent a number of prominent Jews to concentration camps. When we discussed these events at about mid-day at the District Party Leader's home, we concluded that the Jewish question had assumed a completely new perspective. The huge campaign against the Jews on November 10th and on the preceding night served to annul all of the laws and decrees already existing on the subject. We felt – and this was particularly my opinion – that we should now act autonomously.'

At first, Holz suggested to his 'boss' that he use methods to acquire Jewish land and houses as 'legal' as the methods then being adopted to expropriate Jewish shops and businesses. 'We found ourselves in new circumstances,' he continued. 'The Jewish question had been transformed. I am convinced that no National Socialist felt differently at that time.'

The compensation paid by Streicher's organization for expropriated property amounted to ten per cent of its value or of the asking price. Derisory valuations were justified on the grounds that most of the property had been bought during the Great Inflation for less than one-tenth of its value. A search, however, revealed that this was untrue. According to a Treasury Department expert five notaries in Nuremberg and Fürth pocketed some 100,000 marks through transactions of this sort. The first document submitted in evidence of these deals dated from November 10th 1938. It concerned the purchase of movable property belonging to a Jewish congregation by the city of Fürth. The property had been valued at 57,000 marks but was sold for 100 marks. A second document set out the sale of a Jew's (one Sahlmann's) property valued at 1,800 marks for the sum of 180 marks, to the city of Fürth (represented in the transaction by some of its officials). Members of the Bavarian Party acquired some two million marks from forced sales in the period up to December 3rd. The experts on the commission later declared that the real value of the property expropriated amounted to sixteen million marks, given that some of the houses brought in monthly revenues of 30,000–40,000 for their 'new owners', the Nazis, and that the managers of these properties earned monthly salaries of 700–800 marks. Streicher's aide revealed during a hearing before Marshal Goering himself that by the procedure which he had devised, if it had been carried through, nearly thirty million marks would have been amassed in Franconia alone during the next six months.

Streicher enlarged his own personal fortune in order to cover the cost of maintenance of his properties at Nonnenhorn near Lake Constance and at Pleikershof near Fürth. He arranged to acquire Jewish businesses and ordered SA Oberführer Koenig to buy shares worth 112,000 marks in a company called Mars. Martin Kohn, the banker who owned the coveted shares, was detained in preventive custody and compelled to sell them at five per cent. of their nominal value. Deputy District Party Leader Holz made 1,578,000 marks from the sale of thirty-eight Jewish-owned houses and 350 other deals completed in his own name. These were labelled 'unsolicited gifts' and paid into the Communal Bank of Bavaria. Among the many associates of Streicher implicated in the financial scandal by the commission of inquiry there were SA and SS chiefs such as Dr Hahn (a former student of Economics at the University of Grenoble from 1926 to 1928), who was thrice convicted of forging academic diplomas. Also implicated were some group leaders of the Labour Front, as well as municipal councillors, lawyers and even a writer and astrologer, Marie Obermeier, who had been hired to read these gentlemen's horoscopes.

Marshal Goering, whom Hitler had empowered to take action anywhere in the Reich, called a meeting on November 12th 1938 to discuss ways of mastering the anarchy and 'carrying the solution of the Jewish problem to its conclusion in an orderly manner.'[5] On the day official cars arrived one by one at the forecourt of the Air Ministry, carrying the leading figures of the regime. Goering called the meeting to order at eleven o'clock precisely. With him were Dr Goebbels, Walter Funk, Minister of the Economy, Rudolf Brinkmann, Secretary of State for the Ministry of the Economy, the inscrutable and pious Count Schwerin von Krosigk, Minister of Finance, flanked by Karl Blessing, Director of the Bank of the Reich, Wilhelm Frick, Minister of the Interior, and Hans Gürtner, Minister of Justice. Heydrich, Head of Security, also attended, with General Daluege, Chief of Police, Dr Ernst Woermann, who represented the Foreign Ministry, and the District Party Leaders of Austria and the Sudeten Territories.

When he had settled into his armchair, Marshal Goering gave vent to his irritation. The meeting which he had called here a month before to discuss the same subject had had no effect. 'Unfortunately we did no more than dream up brilliant schemes which have been half-heartedly and sluggishly executed.

'The result has been an outbreak of anarchy and chaotic demonstrations. We must act immediately, because, gentlemen, I have had enough of demonstrations. They don't damage the Jews. They damage me. I am responsible for the economy. Whenever a Jewish shop is wrecked and merchandise is scattered in the streets, the insurance companies have to pay damages to the Jews while the public is deprived of the consumer goods which belong to them. If demonstrations are deemed necessary in future, I would ask you to be certain that they do not harm us. It is folly to plunder or burn large Jewish shops for which German insurance companies will have to pay damages. It is folly to burn up entire racks of clothing and other goods which are urgently needed when I shall be made to feel the pinch later on. We might as well go straight ahead and burn up raw materials.'

Turning to face the responsible ministers, Goering added in a conciliatory tone, 'Of course, the people do not know this. And for this reason it is vital to set out clearly in terms of the law what action is being taken to deal with the situation.'

The Marshal indicated that a distinction would have to be made in such legislation between important transactions (among which the confiscation of Jewish companies by the State, and whatever international complications that might entail, took high priority) and spectacular measures which were intended to rally public opinion, such as the 'Aryanization' of the shops which were still in Jewish hands.

'The trouble starts here,' the Marshal stressed, spacing each word. 'On the human level it is easily understandable that we should reward our Party comrades by inviting them to enter into these transactions. But I have witnessed the most rampant abuses: the chauffeurs of some district party leaders, for example, have accumulated fortunes of close on half a million marks. You know what is going on, gentlemen. You know this is so, don't you?' he asked with apparent candour.

Contrary to what had occurred at the previous meeting on October 14th (see page 25), no one dared protest. A murmur of approbation swept across the room. Content with having got his first point across, Goering then proceeded to give a long-winded, emphatic explanation of his scheme for the 'Aryanization' of Jewish companies.[6] These transactions should be treated like any other business transactions, he said, at least as far as the German purchaser was concerned. The government Fiduciary Council would evaluate each Jewish company and the Aryan purchaser would pay that amount to the State. The State would then determine its liability at the lowest possible value, and would record it in the ledger of government debts on behalf of the Jewish proprietor, who would live on the interest accruing from this debt.

As far as foreign Jews were concerned, those who were really foreigners must be treated according to the laws of their own countries. 'But I would ask you not to give any special consideration to Jews who were formerly German, who have always lived in Germany, and who adopted some other nationality in recent years, or does anyone object to this?'

Dr Woermann could not conceal his anxiety and asked, 'I wonder if the Foreign Minister might be consulted in each case, since it is difficult to lay down any general rule.'

Goering : 'We cannot possibly advise you about each separate case, but we shall certainly do so on the category as a whole.'

Dr Woermann, an exacting expert, pressed his point. 'I would like the Foreign Minister to be consulted in each individual case. We cannot be certain what action might be taken.'

Marshal Goering grew impatient with this hair-splitting. 'I do not want a great deal of trouble spent on this category, because I know how much has already been done, particularly in Austria and in the Czech territories. For example, we have no reason to concern ourselves with a Sudeten Jew who was formerly a Czech subject, and there is no need to bother the Foreign Ministry about him, since this territory obviously belongs to us now.

95

'However, in Austria and in the Sudeten territories a substantial number have become English or American or whatever. As a general rule, we cannot take that into consideration.'

Woermann's interjection had cut into the tense solemnity that had dominated the meeting. The servile Minister of the Economy in his turn asked if Jewish shops should be reopened.

'I have already fixed Monday as the day to settle that,' Goebbels riposted, pleased at the chance to outface Marshal Goering.

'That is for me to decide,' Goering broke in angrily.

Unruffled, the propaganda gnome continued. 'Sites released through the demolition of synagogues offer a number of possible uses. Some towns will want to turn them into parking lots or build shops on them. I believe that these circumstances offer an opportunity to dissolve the synagogues entirely. Any which are not completely intact must be evacuated by the Jews at their own expense. Here in Berlin they are ready to do so. The synagogues in the capital which burned down will be cleared by the Jews themselves and replaced by other buildings. This procedure must be adopted throughout Germany.

'I also believe,' Goebbels continued, 'that a decree must be issued excluding Jews from attending theatres, cinemas and German circuses. . . . I think that we can easily afford such a measure because our theatres are recklessly overcrowded as it is. I am of the opinion that we cannot permit Jews to sit down at variety shows or in cinemas or theatres side by side with Germans. We may nevertheless consider a little later the possibility of granting Berlin Jews one or two cinemas in which Jewish films can be shown, but they must not set foot in German theatres.'

Dr Goebbels was manifestly obsessed by the problem of promiscuity. 'It is in any case necessary to exclude Jews from all areas of public life where their presence may have a provocative effect. For example, a Jew is still permitted to share a sleeping compartment in a train with a German. The Minister of Transport must issue instructions for special compartments to be installed for Jews, but only to the extent that such compartments are not required by Germans.'

Mr. de Moro-Giafferi, chief lawyer for Grynszpan's defence.

Herschel Grynszpan, seventeen years old, who shot the Third Secretary at the German embassy, Ernst vom Rath.

Hitler sat in the front row at vom Rath's funeral at Düsseldorf.

...rning of the Great Synagogue
...n.

...windows on the Kurfürsten-
...in Berlin.

...rior of the synagogue in Fa-
...asse in Berlin following the
...struction.

The main synagogue in Frankfurt burned while crowds watched.

The interior of the Magdeburg synagogue after it was dynamited.

Yad Washem Archive, Jerusalem

The Jews were led through the streets of Baden-Baden by the Nazis to the National Hotel. They had to carry a Star of David inscribed "God, do not abandon us."

Zeitgeschichtes Bildarchiv, Munich

Profanation of the scrolls.

The lawyer Hauser, later brutally beaten, was forced to trample on a prayer shawl as he entered the synagogue at Baden-Baden while Nazis stood by and jeered.

Yad Washem Archive, Jerusalem

The interior of the synagogue at Baden-Baden. The SS forced the Jews to sing Nazi songs and to read *Mein Kampf* instead of the Torah (scrolls of the Law) before the Ark.

Yad Washem Archive, Jerusalem

Yad Washem Archive, Jerusalem

he Jews were forced to climb the steps of the synagogue at Baden-Baden hile being beaten by the Nazis.

:ws being arrested after the "Crystal Night."

C.D.J.C., Paris

Bruno Rößler & Blau
Möbel-Fabrik
Teichstr. 5·8

C.D.J.C., Par.

"Jews not wanted here": a Christian shrine in Ba
varia off limits to Jews.

"Jews are not wanted in our German forests." Th
decision was taken at the meeting of Novemb
12th 1938 in Goering's office.

Yad Washem Archive, Jerusalem

"Stand in silence here but do not keep silent whe
you go away": a commemorative monument i
East Berlin. *Yad Washem Archive, Jerusale*

Marshal Goering was growing restless. It seemed obvious that Goebbels wanted to run everything himself. 'It is arrant nonsense to assign special compartments to Jews in proportion to the space available. There must be Jewish carriages. When they are full, the Jews will simply have to stay at home.'

Goebbels, who was not to be defeated, parried the assault. 'It may also be that all the places reserved for Jews will be left unoccupied. Suppose, for example, that there were only two Jews in the Jewish section of a Munich express which was elsewhere full to overflowing. The Jews would hold a privileged position. We must rather lay down that Jews will not be entitled to places until all Germans have claimed theirs.'

Marshal Goering finally lost his temper. 'We don't have to deal with particular situations. We need merely to consider general principles here. If Goebbels' example actually did occur, we wouldn't have to pass a special law : one would simply kick the Jew out even if it meant he had to travel in the toilet.'

The two men found it easier to agree on forbidding Jews access to beaches, pools and country resorts.

'We can either reserve a special beach for them or a few watering places of secondary importance.'

Goering also responded genially to Goebbels' idea of keeping Jews out of German forests. 'We could mark out certain parts of the forests for them which we could populate with animals that resemble them, such as elks which also have hooked noses.'

Goebbels was still worried about promiscuity. He suggested that Jews be forbidden to sit in public parks. 'There are some Jews who don't look Jewish who plonk themselves down beside German mothers and their children and try telling them all sorts of things. I think this is a definite danger and we must therefore reserve special parks for Jews – not the beautiful ones, naturally – and specify which benches they shall be allowed to use.'

Another opportunity for promiscuity occurred in schools. Jewish children should be taken out and put into special schools.

It was getting late. A secretary timidly reminded Marshal Goering that Herr Hilgard had been waiting for him in the antechamber outside since eleven o'clock. Enough of 'cultural interludes': it was time to get down to serious business.

The man who now joined the meeting was a representative of the German insurance companies, many of which would face bankruptcy if they had to pay for all the goods destroyed in the demonstrations.

'Herr Hilgard,' Marshal Goering said, gesturing to a chair. Hilgard bowed courteously to the others. 'This is what we are discussing,' Goering explained. 'The legitimate rage of the German people against the Jews has caused a certain amount of damage throughout the Reich. Some windows were broken. Some businesses and individuals suffered damage. Some synagogues were burnt down. I imagine that a number of these Jews – probably the majority of them – were insured against civil disorders.'

Hilgard: 'Yes.'

'We can conclude then that the German people wished to inflict damage on the Jews by a legitimate act of defence and that the Jews were covered by insurance. The matter can be settled relatively easily, since I have only to order insurance companies not to pay the damages. But I am chiefly interested in something else, and this is why I have asked you to join us. In cases where damages were covered by foreign insurers I should like to collect the payments. I want to discuss with you what means we have of recovering these extra foreign currencies. Instead of being paid to Jews, they can help the German economy. My first question would therefore be whether you think the insurance taken out by the Jews is important.'

Hilgard was a punctilious and exacting businessman. He worried about every detail. Three types of insurance were involved, but insurance against riot or civil disorder was not. The policies involved provided the usual cover for fire, breakage of glass, and theft. There were some claims by Jews, but some had also been made by Aryans whose goods had been damaged. Most of the claims were made under fire policies. The claimants were chiefly Jews, but preliminary investigations revealed that this type of damage had been relatively limited. Claims for broken glass presented a completely different picture. Most of the claimants were Aryan owners of properties let to Jews. This was the case, for example, with most of the large shops in Berlin's Kurfürstendamm.

Goebbels: 'The Jews will have to pay the damages.'

Goering was annoyed. 'That doesn't make sense. We have no raw materials. All our glass comes from abroad and uses up reserves of foreign currencies. It is enough to drive one up the wall.'

Hilgard: 'In fact, the glass used in shop windows comes not from Bohemia but exclusively from Belgium. My initial estimate totals six million marks, Marshal Goering, but it is little more than speculation. That amount of glass is equivalent to half the annual production of the entire Belgian glass industry, which, we believe, will not be able to fill our order for about six months.'

Goering turned nervously towards Goebbels. 'This must be explained to the people.'

Goebbels: 'That is impossible at present.'

Goering grew exasperated: 'But we can't go on like this. We won't be able to hold out.'

Herr Hilgard, who up to this moment had kept out of the discussion, reminded them that he still had not dealt with the third category of insurance: theft insurance.

Goering: 'Does merchandise thrown into the streets and burned fall into this category?'

Hilgard: 'I do not believe so.'

Goering: 'Is it included under policies for civil disorder?'

Hilgard: 'This is precisely the question which we have not yet been able to answer. Can one talk about straightforward theft when a violent burglary has taken place in a domicile or a number of objects have been seized together?'

Goering returned obstinately to his thesis: 'There was civil disorder.'

With equal obstinacy Herr Hilgard reminded him that insurance companies were not concerned with civil disorder as they had gradually excluded it from their policies and liquidated existing cover.

The dialogue of the deaf ran on.

99

Goering: 'From the legal standpoint, however, a civil disorder did take place. No one stole or burgled; but in public, and in broad daylight, mobs destroyed things.'

Hilgard remained calm and meticulous: 'Damages caused by a fight are recognized, but not those caused by riot.'

Goering: 'Are these damages covered by insurance?'

Hilgard: 'Not any longer. To cite a concrete example, there is the case of the jeweller's shop Margraf, Unter den Linden, which was insured by us under a blanket policy, so to speak, covering every possible type of damage. The damages claimed by this shop, which was completely ransacked, amount to 1,700,000 marks.'

Goering swivelled towards General Daluege and the Head of Security: 'An enormous round-up must be organized to find these jewels.'

Police General Daluege: 'I have already issued the order. People are being watched round the clock. According to information which I received yesterday, 150 have already been arrested.'

Goering kept on the track of his own idea: 'Otherwise they will be sold to someone else. If someone goes into a shop with jewels that he claims to have bought, the jewels should be seized at once. They must have been stolen or bought under the counter.'

Heydrich: 'We have confirmed eight hundred cases of depredation throughout the country. Several hundred of the pillagers have been arrested and we are now actually recuperating the lost goods.'

At this distance in time the Security Chief's optimism seems demented. Three weeks after the 'Crystal Night', on November 29th, Hitler's aide and Chief of Staff Rudolf Hess was forced to issue a message[7] through the supreme command of the SA requesting the Party services and organization to return to the Gestapo 'the valuables which had to be placed in safety for protection of German property' and to offer their complete support to the police in rounding up thieves.

Goering insisted on his point: 'And what about the jewels?'

Heydrich was embarrassed: 'It is hard to say. Some were thrown into the street where people picked them up. The same sort of thing happened with furs. In Berlin, for example, in the Friedrichstrasse district, crowds threw themselves at the minks and skunks and whisked them off. It is extremely difficult to get these things back. Some children crammed things into their pockets just for the fun of it. We should recommend that the Hitler Youth not be involved in this type of operation without prior notification to the Party.'

Police General Daluege: 'The Party absolutely must order everyone to inform the Police if a neighbour's wife – everyone keeps tabs on his neighbours – suddenly acquires a fur or starts wearing new jewellery.'

Herr Hilgard was slightly impatient at the policemen's dialogue. He wanted to continue the discussion of payments for damages. 'If we refuse now to fulfil our obligations under legal contracts, the honour of German insurance companies will be irrevocably tarnished.'

Goering reassured him. 'Not if I intervene with a government decree or a law.'

Hilgard: 'I was just coming to that.'

Heydrich: 'One could pay the insurance and then confiscate it, so saving appearances.'

Hilgard assented. 'I think Obergruppenführer Heydrich's proposal is a good one. The insurance companies should be used initially to assess the damages and to settle them, but they should be given the chance to pay the premiums into a fund.'

Goering did not find this solution neat enough. 'Just a moment, Herr Hilgard. We will have to settle with the Germans who suffered damages, but you will have an injunction against paying damages directly to the Jews. These indemnities will be paid to the Minister of Finance.'

Herr Hilgard was mildly disconcerted by this. 'Well . . . '

Goering: 'What the Minister of Finance does with the money is his affair.'

The inscrutable Minister of Finance, Count Schwerin von Krosigk, did not stir. He let the experts debate the cost of replacing broken glass.

Herr Hilgard: 'Allow me to add that according to my estimates the total damages throughout Germany amount to about twenty-five million marks. And this is a conservative estimate.'

It was much too conservative for Security Chief Heydrich. 'We assess the damage to goods, stock and merchandise at several hundred millions,' he said. 'This includes the tax loss on the remaining merchandise, capital and income.'

The Minister of Finance found these estimates slightly fantastic. He haughtily broke his silence. 'We haven't the slightest notion of the extent of the damage.'

'But,' Heydrich replied, refusing to be brushed aside, 'five hundred shops in the Reich were destroyed.'

Police General Daluege was not to be left out. 'We must also consider the merchandise which had already arrived in the shops but was still on the accounts of suppliers. Some of them are Aryans who delivered merchandise on consignment.'

Hilgard: 'These goods must be paid for.'

Goering's excitement rekindled. 'I should prefer that you kill two hundred Jews rather than destroy such assets.'

'But thirty-five were killed,' Heydrich parried.

Walter Funk, the habitually servile Minister of the Economy, felt that his colleagues were mistaken. 'If the Jews are forced to pay, the insurance companies will not be obliged to pay anything.'

Goering: 'Exactly, gentlemen. It's as clear as day. We endorse this suggestion. All of the insurers – with the exception of Herr Hilgard, who is here – believe they will have to cover the damages. They actually wish to do so and their attitude is completely understandable. They must not be put in the situation of being unable to uphold their obligations. . . . I think therefore that damages should be assessed and the insurance companies should pay as much as the law obliges them to pay. . . . Let us see what the different types of damages are. First there are damages to Jews, the disappearance of Margraf's jewellery, etc. The jewellery has disappeared and we cannot replace it. Any jewellery found by the police will be forfeited to the State. As to the other things, merchandise thrown into the streets or stolen or burned, the Jews will also have to bear the damages. As for merchandise bought on consignment, the Jews will have to settle for what has been lost.'

Goebbels: 'There is no point in spelling all this out in the decree. A general decree will be perfectly adequate.'

Herr Hilgard was struck with a new worry: 'I'm just wondering to what extent international insurance companies are involved.'

Goering peremptorily announced: 'They will have to pay and we will confiscate the money.'

Hilgard took up his suggestion: 'I imagine that an American or a British supplier of furs on commission would previously have insured them through a British or American company——'

Goebbels: 'The money will be paid to the State one way or another.'

Goering: 'Obviously. The Aryan will not declare damages because the Jews will cover them. The Jews will have to declare the damages. They will recover the insurance payment and we will confiscate it. In the final count the insurance companies will enjoy the benefits because they will not have to pay for all the damages. You can be glad, Herr Hilgard.'

Hilgard's tone became pained. 'I don't see what benefit there is in not having to pay certain damages.'

Goering was by now carried away. 'Please, please. If you are legally obliged to pay out five million and suddenly an angel of mercy resembling my somewhat corpulent form appears to you and says that you can keep a million of it, surely you would benefit, wouldn't you? You might realize that we were splitting fifty-fifty, but you need only consider your own point of view. You would be delighted. You would have a miraculous advantage.'

Herr Hilgard appeared not to relish Goering's sense of humour. He had come, he explained solemnly, to represent the interests of honourable German businessmen, not to mention those of the insured parties who, as a result of this incident, would be obliged to pay higher premiums while receiving smaller dividends.

Goering, who was openly enraged, gestured to Hilgard that his presence was no longer needed. 'In that case,' he said, 'be certain that fewer windows are broken in future. After all, you are one of the people. You should send your representatives around to make them understand. And that is that.'

Herr Hilgard gave a dignified nod round the table and left.

The discussion turned to the problem of foreign Jews. Dr Woermann, from the Foreign Ministry, was as meticulous in his domain as Herr Hilgard had been in his. He asked that Goering's decree should be revised so as to specify the fate of foreign Jews. Heydrich, who wanted to avoid further legal hair-splitting, proposed that the degree should not be made more specific and that the foreign Jews' property be confiscated without warning.

Goering, an orderly man, objected. 'No, you cannot behave in that way. The law must be clearly intelligible. Contrary to Dr Woermann's suggestion, however, we need only concern ourselves with uninsured foreign Jews, who must be the exceptions.'

Woermann's tone became concerned. 'We could be deluged with claims.'

Goering: 'I should like to avoid a great deal of attention being drawn to foreign Jews.'

Woermann was obdurate: 'Since it is dealt with in Article 2 it could also be mentioned in Article 1. The Minister of Justice's first proposal was more satisfactory.'

Here discussion of this point ended. They then turned to the Austrian problem. The ministerial adviser Fischboeck had vehemently protested at the previous meeting against Goering's accusation that Austrian leaders had turned the Aryanization of Jewish property into a 'charitable operation for incompetent Nazis'. Now, however, he was radiant. He would prove to his German masters that the Austrians were better organized than the Germans.

'Field-Marshal Goering, we have already worked out a detailed plan for Austria. In Vienna there are 12,000 artisan businesses and 5,000 Jewish shops. A comprehensive plan for these 17,000 businesses was drafted before the National Socialist revolution took place. It had been decided to shut 10,000 of the artisan businesses and to keep 2,000. Of the 5,000 shops, we expected to transfer 1,000 to Aryans and to shut 4,000. According to this plan 3,000 or 3,500 businesses would be left, depending on local and professional requirements. Our plan will be made practicable by a law which we first requested as long ago as last September. . . . The text can be kept short.'

Goering: 'I'll draw up the decree today.'

Fischboeck explained that the decree would permit the removal of the last vestige of Jewish business in Austria by the end of 1938.

Goering: 'That will be excellent. This is a commendable proposition. Between now and Christmas, or the beginning of the year, we can settle the matter in Vienna, which is one of the bastions of Jewry.'

Walter Funk, the Minister of the Economy, felt that his Austrian colleague was displaying too much initiative. 'We could do the same in Germany,' he rebutted in an irritated tone. 'I have already drawn up an ordinance prohibiting Jews from carrying on any retail or mail-order business after January 1st 1939. They are also forbidden to employ anyone for this purpose or to accept orders. . . . After the same date Jews will not be allowed to conduct business as defined in the law regulating national labour of January 20th 1934. . . . Jews will not be allowed to belong to co-operatives. . . . The relevant German ministers will be empowered to devise ways of applying this ordinance.'

Goering glowed with satisfaction. 'I believe we can sign this ordinance. . . .' (General approbation and cries of 'Hear, hear!') 'It all seems extremely well prepared.'

The expert Schmer thought it necessary to add a few details. 'Personally I think our Aryanization programme has been successful so far. We shall have no difficulty in finding buyers for the few businesses we may wish to keep open. The premises of the others can easily be rented out, especially in Berlin, where demand is heavy.'

Goering: 'But, my friend, in that case the Jews will pocket the entire value of the sale.'

Schmer: 'They will receive a sum very much lower than the real value, since Aryanization will continue to be under our control.'

Goering continued: 'You mean the sums will be paid directly to the Jews rather than being entered on the register of public debts?'

Schmer grew impatient: 'Not at all, one needn't bother. They won't be able to spend the money. The money will be frozen anyway, since Jews are obliged to declare any alteration in their personal assets. These are constantly registered. The money cannot slip past us. It will remain in Germany. You need only draft a new decree or delegate the powers granted to the Minister of the Economy in Article 7.[8] The money can't possibly slip past us.'

Goering was not convinced. 'But, Herr Schmer, suppose the beneficiary of Aryanization receives thirty thousand marks. All he has to do is run to the nearest corner, buy some jewels and cross the border on the same day.'

Schmer remained impassive. 'He is nevertheless obliged to declare the change in his assets.'

Goering was beside himself. 'But suppose he clears out.'

Fischboeck, who was delighted to have the chance to demonstrate Austrian efficiency, assumed the role of peacemaker. 'The price of the transaction need not be paid when Aryanization takes place. In Austria the amount will be paid in instalments over a long period if the buyer cannot pay cash. If he pays in cash the money is initially paid into a frozen account.'

This reassured Goering. 'We can also do that.'

Schmer: 'The authorizing decree can stipulate that money over a certain amount shall be paid as a loan to the State or something similar. An order to the relevant offices will suffice. . . . Should the Austrians keep their regulations?'

Goering: 'Yes, just as they are.'

Fischboeck: 'Except that we can block everything. We are particularly concerned about Jewish apartment houses, which constitute a sizeable proportion of Jewish property. While the cash assets declared in Austria amount to only 320 million marks,[9] the value of apartment houses alone amounts to 500 million marks. We would like the decree authorizing the expropriation of Jewish assets to apply to apartment houses. We can then put them in the hands of an administrator and give the Jews government bonds. . . .'

There was also the question of stocks and shares. In Austria these made up a large part of Jewish assets: about 226 million marks. Fischboeck recommended that they be exchanged for government bonds costing the Minister of Finance 3 per cent interest.

Walter Funk had been sharply annoyed by his Austrian colleague. 'Why shouldn't the Jews be entitled to have bills of credit?'

Goering: 'They would then be indirectly associated with the German economy.'

Funk: 'But this is an entirely different matter.'

Goering broke in: 'No, I was perfectly clear about stocks and shares a moment ago.'

Funk: 'Stocks and shares, not government debts.'

Fischboeck wanted to have the last word. 'It is nevertheless better to pay 3 per cent to a Jew than 4.5 per cent, and it would be impossible to control Jewish assets if one issued bills of credit.'

Goering's tone became sharp. 'Gentlemen, let us have no further discussion. Jews are not allowed to keep bills. They must surrender them.'

Fischboeck began sketching out a plan for redeeming the bills. But the Minister of the Economy replied banteringly, 'So that the Reich will gain title to 500 million shares.'

Goering: 'Wonderful.'

Goebbels came to the rescue. 'If necessary, the government can sell them.'

Fischboeck: 'It could be quite profitable.'

The Minister of Finance, Count Schwerin von Krosigk, haughtily intervened for the second time since the meeting had begun. 'I'm wondering first of all if there would be an advantage. Even if we allow that there would be, the result is a completely different arrangement. I can see very clearly what Minister Fischboeck has in mind. It is an entirely new idea to dispossess Jews' bonds when we originally wanted to let them keep title to their income.'

Fischboeck defended his project. 'This is a very important part of the whole plan, since the Jews will otherwise retain possession of easily convertible assets which they can use in other ways.'

Goering: 'That is very true. We do not want to give the Jews any chance of conniving against us.'

Fischboeck grew increasingly inflamed. He suggested that the Jews be divested of their jewels so that they would be left with nothing other than government bonds.

Heydrich: 'Could we not issue a general order prohibiting them from investing what money they have in specific articles, such as works of art, for example?'

Goering: 'The rules for entering names on the register of public debts are very much simpler. The bonds are non-transferable and they would not be able to do a great deal with them. They won't go very far on 3.5 per cent either.'

Heydrich: 'We must also do something to control the surrender of what the Jews have in their possession.'

Goering: 'What they have at this moment. We're just getting to that.'

Schmer: 'Article 7 of your decree[10] refers to full powers to use Jewish property for the benefit of the German economy within the framework of the Four Year Plan.'

Goering suggested setting up a select committee to carry out the points discussed. Wilhelm Frick, Minister of the Interior, who had been silent until then, asked to be a member of it, but Goering wanted to keep it as small as possible.

Buerkel, the District Party Leader of the Sudeten territories, also spoke up. 'Will it also deal with the Aryanization plan?'

Goering pounced on him as if he were a naughty schoolboy. 'But the whole matter revolves around this plan, which will be worked out by Herr Fischboeck. All the same, I hope that you have followed and absorbed enough to understand everything that concerns the Sudeten population.'

Turning to the others, he added, 'I believe, of course, that the economic measures will have to be buttressed with a series of police actions, propaganda and cultural measures, so that it is all made perfectly clear and so that Judaism will be struck one blow after another, bang, bang, bang.'

Obergruppenführer Heydrich, inspired by these last words, followed on. 'You are perfectly right, Field-Marshal. The exclusion of Jews from the economy does not resolve the basic problem. The Jews must leave Germany. May I make a few proposals?

'On the instruction of the German High Commissioner, we have established a centralized Jewish emigration service in Vienna, thanks to which we have disencumbered Austria of fifty thousand Jews, while the Reich has oñly managed to get rid of nineteen thousand during the same period.'

Goering did not wish to be brushed aside. 'Most of the time you have had to collaborate with local commanders at the frontiers to arrange illegal crossings.'

Heydrich: 'In only a tiny fraction of cases, Field-Marshal. Illegal emigrants——'

Goering broke in. 'The story was in all the papers. The first night the Jews were deported into Czechoslovakia. The following morning the Czechs took them and sent them on to Hungary. Hungary sent them back to Germany and Czechoslovakia, and so on from country to country. Finally they wound up on an old barge in the Danube. They had to settle there. When they tried to land they were repulsed.'

Heydrich was irritated. 'That incident involved a hundred Jews.'

Goering: 'In actual fact for a fortnight a certain number of Jews from Burgenland crossed the border at midnight.'

Heydrich grey emphatic. 'Legal measures have permitted the emigration of 45,000 Jews.'

Goering: 'How did you go about it?'

Heydrich: 'We required wealthy Jews who wanted to emigrate to deposit a certain sum of money with their Jewish congregation. This money and payments in foreign currencies subsequently financed the emigration of the poorer Jews. It was not so much a problem of getting rid of rich Jews as of getting rid of the Jewish rabble.'

Goering: 'My dear children, do you really think that we can get by with getting rid of a few hundred thousand of this rabble. Has it ever for a moment occurred to you that this procedure is going to cost so much in foreign credits that it will prove impracticable?'

Heydrich: 'It will cost no more than the foreign currencies which each Jew receives.'

Goering: 'Agreed.'

'Therefore,' Heydrich continued, 'I suggest that a similar service be established in Germany and that we hammer out a solution based on the procedure I have mentioned, but incorporating Field-Marshal Goering's very valuable criticism.'

Goering: 'Agreed.'

Heydrich: 'Secondly, to be rid of the Jews we shall need an emigration programme covering at least eight or ten years. We shall not be able to get more than eight thousand to ten thousand to leave annually. A certain number will still be with us. Aryanization and other restrictions on their activities will reduce Judaism to destitution, and we shall see the proletarianization of the Jews who remain. I shall therefore have to implement measures in Germany which will isolate Jews from normal spheres of activity on the one hand, while on the other I have to find a way of limiting Jews' occupations to definite fields of action such as the law, medicine, hairdressing and so on. This question must be gone into. As far as the isolation of the Jews is concerned, I should like simply to mention a few measures, which have to do only with the police, but which are important because of their psychological effect on the population. For example, we could oblige all Jews – as defined by the Nuremberg laws – to wear distinguishing insignia. This will simplify matters, particularly our relations with foreign Jews.'

Goering was thrilled. 'Yes, or a uniform.'

Heydrich preferred an insignia. 'It will avoid involving foreign Jews who are protected by their governments.'

Goering: 'But, my dear Heydrich, in the long run you can't avoid creating ghettoes in the cities. They are bound to be created.'

Heydrich: 'I'm just coming to that. If by "ghettoes" you mean areas restricted to Jews, it seems to me that the police would find them unmanageable, because they will leave Jews free to band together with one another. It would be too difficult to keep tabs on them. Such ghettoes would breed crime, epidemics and other such problems.

These days the German population itself – we shall not allow the Jews to live in the same houses as Germans – compels the Jews to keep to their own houses and to the streets where they live. The vigilant eye of the entire population is more effective in restricting the Jews than any attempt to assemble thousands of Jews in a particular section of a city, where their surveillance by uniformed law officers could not be guaranteed.'

Goering: 'You need only cut the telephone connections with the outside.'

Heydrich: 'I could not prevent all contact with the outside, however.'

Goering: 'And what about special cities?'

Heydrich: 'This is a possibility. But such cities would be centres of delinquency and inevitably very dangerous. I would do something else. We could place certain zones out of bounds to Jews: for example, the government and residential sections of Munich.'

Goering: 'Stop there. I'm rather less worried about setting eyes on Jews where I don't want to than I am about reducing them to subsistence level. With the 3.5 per cent interest which they receive they will not be able to be extravagant – in restaurants, and so on. They will have to work harder and this will produce a higher concentration that is easier to control. We will know that a particular building is entirely inhabited by Jews. We shall also have to assemble Jewish butchers, hairdressers, grocers, in Jewish streets. However, we must also decide whether we want to allow this. Otherwise, Jews will have to buy from Aryans.'

Heydrich: 'In my opinion it would be better if Germans could avoid serving Jews for ordinary everyday things.'

Goering: 'But wait. You can't just let them die of hunger, and this presents a problem. If you allow Jews to keep a certain number of retail shops, they will still be involved in trade and there will also have to be wholesalers.'

Schmer: 'That will not be possible in small towns.'

Goering continued, 'It will only be possible if you set aside entire areas or even entire towns for Jews. Otherwise we shall have to decide that only Germans can run businesses and the Jews will have to buy from Germans. They have to be able to buy food, shoes and socks.'

Heydrich: 'We must decide.'

Goering: 'I would like to take the decision today. We can't go back to fiddling with distinctions. We can't say that the Jews will be allowed to run this or that shop simply because we can't check up. They will also need wholesale shops. Therefore all shops must be Aryan. The Jews can buy from them. Eventually we can take another step and decree that particular shops will be reserved for them. We can also allow a few Jewish barbers. We may allow them to have certain jobs in certain specific streets, but not to run shops.'

Heydrich: 'How would one do this in a ghetto? Would Jews have to do their shopping in the Aryan sections?'

Goering: 'No. I'm sure that there are more than enough German shopkeepers who would groan with pleasure if they could set up shop in a ghetto. In any case, I shall not depart from the policy that there is no longer room for Jews in the economy.'

Heydrich tentatively suggested, 'I should prefer not to decide. There are still some important psychological points.'

Goering returned to his idea: 'When we have set the ghettoes up we can decide what shops should be allowed and we can say to a specific group of Jews: You, Jews, can have the concession for deliveries. A German company will furnish the goods. The Jews will not have shops but will operate consumer co-operatives for Jews.'

Heydrich: 'In actual practice, all these measures are leading towards a ghetto. It seems to me that we shouldn't set up ghettoes now. All these measures will inevitably force the Jews into ghettoes in the way we have discussed.'

The Minister of the Economy, Funk: 'The Jews will have to help each other out. Unless they look after each other they will die of hunger.'

Goering: 'First let us consider what Minister Goebbels suggested a moment ago: obligatory resettlement and the concentration of Jewish outlets.'

Heydrich was annoyed at not being allowed to complete his

proposal. 'I should also like to propose that all personal authorizations, such as passes and driving licences, be withdrawn from Jews. Jews should no longer be allowed to endanger German lives by owning or driving cars. On the other hand their movements will have to be restricted by regulations against entering certain buildings, such as the Royal Square in Munich. Jews will have to be excluded from a certain area surrounding important government buildings. The same regulations should apply to cultural institutions, border areas, and military camps. And, as Minister Goebbels has just suggested, they should also be excluded from theatres, cinemas and so on. As to cures, I think it should be remembered that a visit to a watering place is a luxury and not an absolute necessity. Millions of German citizens have no chance to improve their health by visiting watering places. I can't see any reason why Jews should be allowed to take the waters.'

Goering: 'Not in watering places.'

Heydrich: 'In that case, I would suggest the same for hospitals. A Jew cannot be allowed to occupy a bed in a hospital beside Aryan citizens.'

Goering: 'We shall have to arrive at this gradually.'

Heydrich: 'The same with public transport.'

Goering: 'Aren't there Jewish sanatoriums and hospitals——' (Interruption: 'Of course, Yes.') 'All of this will have to be gone into and decrees issued one by one.'

Heydrich: 'I simply wanted to arrive at an agreement in principle so that we can begin to set this on foot.'

Goering: 'One more question, gentlemen. Do you think I can announce today that the Jews will have to pay a 1,000 million mark fine?'

District Party Leader Buerckel: 'The Viennese would support such a measure wholeheartedly.'

Goebbels (doubtful): 'I wonder if the Jews will find a way to evade it by putting something aside.'

Brinkmann (legalising): 'But they will fall foul of the law.'

The Minister of Finance, Count Schwerin von Krosigk, now condescended to address his Austrian colleague. 'I have one question,

Herr Fischboeck. Can one order such a payment without at the same time forbidding them to liquidate assets? There is a risk that the Jews will put their loans on the market.'

Funk was annoyed at not being consulted. 'But they have declared everything, including cash assets.'

Schwerin von Krosigk contributed punctiliously: 'They are allowed to make short-term use of them.'

Goering turned sardonic. 'What good would it do to convert them into money if they can't use them?'

Funk replied sententiously: 'If they sell the bonds they will suffer a loss.'

Fischboeck: 'There is that risk, but it is not a great one as long as other measures are taken during the course of next week.'

Schwerin von Krosigk continued being punctilious. 'The measures must be taken next week at the latest.'

Goering: 'That is what I would insist upon.'

Fischboeck: 'Perhaps it is a good way of setting ourselves a deadline.'

Goering rubbed his hands. 'I should prefer that the draft of the decree announced that the German Jews are to be fined 1,000 million marks for their nefarious crime. It will cause a stir. Those pigs will think twice before they commit another murder. Once again I am forced to admit that I should not like to be a Jew in Germany.'

Count Schwerin von Krosigk, who now became markedly loquacious, tried to give the discussion a more dignified tone. 'For this reason I should like strongly to emphasise what Herr Heydrich said at the very outset. We must use every possible means, with the expedient of permitting Jews to take more property with them, to get them out of the country. It is essential that the proletariat not be left behind, since their upkeep would be a formidable burden.'

The Minister of the Interior, Frick: 'And dangerous.'

Schwerin von Krosigk: 'Confinement in a ghetto is not a pleasurable prospect. Our object must therefore be, as Heydrich indicated, to make as many as possible leave.'

Goering's tone became menacing. 'One more point. If the Reich were to be involved in an international conflict in the near future, it goes without saying that our first task would be to settle accounts with the Jews remaining in Germany. And one more point. Through diplomatic channels the Führer is going to approach, in the first instance, the Powers which raised the Jewish problem so as to arrive at a settlement of the Madagascar question.[11] He spoke to me at length about it on November 9th. No other solution is left. He wants to tell the rest of the world, "Why are you always talking about the Jews? You take them." There is another solution. The rich Jews could buy a large territory in North America or Canada or somewhere else for their fellow Jews. To sum up, the Minister of the Economy will chair the committee which we have agreed to set up and will implement our decisions here in the next few days.'

Blessing, Director of the Reichsbank: 'I'm afraid that starting on Monday and in the next few days the Jews may want to sell government bonds worth hundreds of thousands of marks in order to have cash. Since we plan to raise loans in future, the loan consortium – that is to say, the Minister of Finance – will have to accept these bonds.'

Goering: 'How will Jews set about putting bonds on the open market?'

'By selling them.'

Goering: 'To whom?'

'On the stock market. They issue instructions to a bank.'

Goering: 'In that case the matter is easy to deal with. I'll block the sale of government bonds for three days.'

Blessing responded legalistically: 'It will have to be decided in an ordinance.'

Goering: 'But I can't see how the Jews will benefit. They have no idea how much they are going to have to pay. They are more likely to sit tight.'

Goebbels replied sententiously: 'For the moment they are small and ugly and stay at home.'

Goering: 'I can't see any point. Otherwise the decree will have to be issued. I want the decree to be published immediately. The situation has settled down now, but who can guarantee that there won't be another incident on Saturday or Sunday? Above all, any sudden movement must be avoided. The Reich has taken the matter in hand. The Jews can sell things, but what will they do then? They will still have to hand the money over to us. No matter what, they will have to pay. And then they will have no way of knowing how much they will be assessed for. The Jews will not dream of putting anything on the market to start with. I know them. They will begin jabbering, then they'll flock to our offices, and so on. Then they'll go to see influential Aryans with the hope of obtaining favours. They'll see the so-called "Reich letter-boxes" with various orders in which they can express their grievances. Finally they will besiege me. It will all take a lot of time. And we can see to it.'

The meeting had lasted for three hours. It was 2.40 in the afternoon. The hushed murmurs of the smoke-filled room had gradually swelled to an uproar. Everyone wanted to declaim his own ideas, his own arguments. Portly Marshal Goering mopped his brow. He was evidently tired. 'Gentlemen, I can only thank you. The meeting is over.'

5

The Camps

While the German masters debated the most effective ways of depriving the Jews of their last possessions, some thirty thousand Jews, men of between sixteen and eighty years old, were arrested and taken to concentration camps in response to Müller's Gestapo teletype message and Security Chief Heydrich's instructions for the 'Crystal Night' operation.

In the days after November 10th buses and trains carried 10,911 Jews from various cities in the South of Germany and Austria to Dachau, 9,845 Jews from Central Germany to Buchenwald, and 9,000 Jews from Prussia and the Baltic coast to Sachsenhausen.[1]

At this time neither the older camps, Dachau and Sachsenhausen, which had been opened almost at the advent of National Socialism, nor the camp at Buchenwald, built in 1937 on the Thuringian hill of Ettersberg to receive detainees from central Germany, operated as the mammoth 'death factories' that Treblinka, Maïdanek and Auschwitz were later to become. They had been set up in order to 'silence by terror' the German adversaries of Nazism, the Jews and the 'anti-social types'. They were also used as a testing ground for the system and as something closely resembling training centres for professional torturers.

Dachau,[2] the oldest of the three camps, was delightfully situated on the outskirts of Munich. Jewish detainees were received under blinding spotlights by ranks of hundreds of armed and helmeted SS troopers. Some of the exhausted men fainted under the searing violence of the lights. A rabbi among the new arrivals recited the prayer of the dead. The prisoners of 'Operation Crystal Night' (many of whom were under seventeen or over seventy) were kept standing without food for eight hours while they underwent admission formalities. Their heads were shorn and they passed through alternately icy and scalding showers. This was the first display of SS sadism. The majority of the SS guards, excluding the commandant, were under twenty-two years old. They asked questions while the prisoners were being showered and shot streams of icy water into their mouths as they struggled to answer. When the striped uniforms were handed out, the guards took obvious delight in dressing the fat prisoners in uniforms that were too tight.

The men were divided up two hundred to a dormitory. Regardless of age or health, they were obliged to rise at half-past four in the morning. They were given half an hour to wash and queue up for the W.C. before roll-call. There was a second roll-call in the evening. Breakfast consisted of a hot chicory drink and black bread. Lunch comprised vegetables with a few splinters of meat, and rice or tapioca with milk. Supper consisted of soup and a hunk of rye bread with a sliver of sausage or cheese. Sometimes the soup was replaced by a herbal tea. The 'November Jews' wore a distinguishing Star of David composed of a yellow lower triangle and a red upper triangle. This was the badge worn by 'political prisoners'. The other Jews, most of whom had been arrested during the round-ups in the summer of 1938, wore a Star of David with a yellow lower triangle and a black upper triangle: the insignia of 'anti-social' prisoners. They were made to do 'limbering-up exercises' until mid-day and again after the lunch break until five in the evening. There was no remission for illness or weakness. When a seventy-year-old Jewish inmate, who was a doctor, called on a German 'colleague' for help, he was asked, 'What's the matter with you, you dirty old Jew?'

The old man was shocked and tried to explain his case. By way of examination, his 'colleague' asked him to turn round, landed a heavy kick, and added, 'Filthy pig, you're just lazy!'

Everyone received the same treatment, including such dignitaries as Aufhäuser, a banker from Munich, whose brother, a naturalized Englishman, acted as the Swedish Consul General in Munich, or Baron Hirsch, a Catholic convert who was made to watch his castle at Planegge burn, while his porcelain collection, valued at a million marks and willed to a German museum, was destroyed.

The Adjutant Commander of the camp was incontestably the most inspired torturer. He trampled prisoners under foot and had them flogged with a whip.

Brutality at Dachau was, however, no worse than at Sachsenhausen.[3] The Jews from Prussia and the Baltic coast were greeted by high, long barbed-wired fences and walls surmounted by searchlights and watchtowers. The camp lay in a bleak tract of Brandenburg only about thirty kilometres from Berlin, but the prisoners had little time to spend contemplating the desolation of their surroundings.

'Run, you Jewish scum! Faster, you bunch of layabouts,' barked an SS trooper as he brandished a riding whip.

'Halt! Stop, you stupid Jews!' another shouted.

'Clear off, you synagogue cattle, or I'll fire in your pious faces!' a third howled.

'Will no one help this dying Jew?'

'So much the better if one of the pigs drops dead now. They'll all drop eventually. They just have to wait their turn. We have something special for each of you. Don't worry. Not bullets, that wouldn't do. We have our means.'

'There we were, trapped in barbed wire,' recalled a survivor.[4] 'Over there, just a few feet away, was the world. Here our minds were vacant, our eyes were unfocused. We lived in torpor. We seemed to stop thinking. The mind only functioned unconsciously. We stood for hours at a stretch. Then knee-bends, curses, hunger, thirst, and more knee-bends.'

'Lower, you scum, lower! Lower! Filthy pigs, read out the words on the board.'

'Wek... Wek...'

'Louder, you bastards!'

'We killed Secretary vom Rath!'

Several hundred voices sang out the syllables together in the night. The yard was filled with men who had often been beaten to a pulp. A rabbi was handed a placard that read, 'I am a traitor and share the guilt for vom Rath's death.' He had to hold it up for twelve hours as he paced across the yard. Now and then someone slumped in a faint. There was no one to look after him: one Jew among many. The SS, troopers trained in the Ordensburgen, most of them under twenty-one, unleashed their violence on the old, the fat, those whose features were pronouncedly semitic or who looked like professional men. They were more civil to the young athletic-looking men and appeared even to enjoy their contact with them.[5]

Someone slit his wrists with a razor. Blood spurted out, Jewish blood. A passing SS trooper grinned and smashed the poor man's jaw with the butt of his revolver. Blood oozed from his face. After a few moments the man collapsed, groaned, gasped and it was over. The stars gleamed in the darkness overhead. Heaven and hell share a common frontier.

'While I was standing in the Appelplatz with these six or seven thousand Jews in semi-military uniforms,' another Sachsenhausen survivor wrote,[6] 'a strange thought suddenly occurred to me. I suddenly realized that I belonged to the largest single concentration of Jewish paramilitary forces anywhere in the world. Arms in the hands of but a few of us and we would cease being defenceless victims at our persecutors' mercy. The sailors on the *Potemkin* must have felt the same sense of humiliation, but they did have arms to crush their enemies. This concentration in itself gave us each a feeling of security which we could not have felt on our own.'

'We must have reached the camp at about ten at night,' another Sachsenhausen survivor recalled.[7]

In the darkness, pierced from time to time by the sweeping arc-lamps, I could make out two to three thousand men arranged in ranks ten deep. I found out later that they had been standing there since their arrival earlier in the day or, in some cases, the night before. We lined up with them and remained on our feet – except for a few brief rests – until half-past two or half-past three the following morning. After the uniforms had been handed out and our heads and beards had been shaven, we took cold showers and returned to 'roll-call' until evening. In all, we were on our feet for 19 hours without a morsel to eat. While the SS guards went off for a moment, the political prisoners assigned to help them slipped us a bit of water while warning us to maintain our military posture.

The SS killed time by howling insults at us. These were often related to the profession or condition of the victim, who had previously been interrogated. Sometimes they kicked prisoners or lashed them across their faces with riding crops.

From the outset we felt that humiliating treatment was meted out to us simply to break us down. Inmates were made to chew and swallow the crumbs of bread that fell on to the ground. Others had to carry placards inscribed, 'We are the destroyers of German civilization.'

'Occasionally we were made to chant slogans in unison. The SS were specially fond of reminding us that we had been annihilated once and for all. They alluded in ironical comments to the perpetual detention of Jews now that the Nazis wielded law and power. One of them, who boasted the nickname 'the Satan of Oranienburg', promised to uphold his reputation in dealing with us.

One incident provided a striking example of the terror which the SS sought to inspire. In the group in front of me were a number of intellectuals: doctors, judges, rabbis, as well as a former public prosecutor, Guggenheim. When he announced his name and occupation he was first interrogated about his income, as we all were, about the importance of his home and the size of his pension. The SS interrogator told Guggenheim what he had told everyone, that he was a broken man and had lost everything. Then he realized that the prosecutor must have known him before he retired. 'Tell me,' he asked, 'Don't we know each other? Didn't you lock up five of my friends in 1930?'

The ex-prosecutor was disconcerted and replied that he could not recall.

'But of course,' the SS interrogator urged. 'We often wondered, in fact, what had happened to you. We've been on the look-out for you for a long time, but we'll settle our score with you now.'

At about eight in the morning the camp commandant came to inspect us with his adjutant. He asked when we had arrived but gave no hint that our interminable wait on the Appelplatz was about to end. Then his eye caught a piece of paper on the ground. He wheeled round to his adjutant and remarked sourly, 'These good-for-nothings don't seem to respect order and cleanliness. We shall have to teach them a lesson.'

Our names were not registered until 1 the following morning. Then there was another long wait, with new discomforts. At about half-past three in the afternoon we were led into the showers. My neighbour, thinking the guards could not see him, put his hat on his head so as to free his hands for undressing. He soon regretted it. An SS trooper whom he had failed to see landed a punch on his head that sent his hat flying. 'Dirty Jew, say that you are a dirty Jew.' Despite the pain, my neighbour tried to remain dignified. He answered precisely with a firm voice, 'I am a Jew.' He was hit again, harder this time, and the order was repeated. They repeated this ritual three or four times, the prisoner replying each time in the same dignified tone, 'I am a Jew.' The SS trooper muttered menacingly but turned on his heels.

While the SS treated the Jews with such crudeness and brutality, the political prisoners, most of whom were communists who had been interned since 1933, tried to mitigate the discomforts of the concentration camp by showing the new arrivals how to deal with them.

Despite the great deference which the Germans normally reserved for military exploits, the Jewish veterans received no special consideration. None of them was asked about his military career either on arrival or subsequently. The camp authorities merely announced that they would have to surrender any civil or military decorations with their money and other valuables. When one detainee handed in two Iron Crosses first and second class, awarded him in the First World War, as well as a decoration for wounds received in action, an SS trooper commented, 'You'll earn another medal for being wounded here.'

Sachsenhausen, which followed the pattern of the early German concentration camps, was divided into three sections. Two of these were outside the main camp and comprised office buildings and workshops and the commandant's and guard's lodgings. The third part, the internal part, was reserved for prisoners. About sixty or seventy barracks, built of wooden planks, were arranged in several rows around the central 'Appelplatz'. Each of the barracks consisted of two day-rooms and two night rooms with a washroom and lavatories and had been designed to accommodate 150 inmates. Although other detainees were assigned 150 to a hut, 300–450 'November Jews' were crammed into each of the huts allotted to them. Whenever Jewish prisoners were released or died, their groups were rearranged in order to obtain the same number. Hygiene was thus precarious. The Jews slept on loose straw at first, later on straw mattresses, with two covers each on average. The so-called infirmary comprised two huts, these also contained the kitchen, the storerooms and the showers, which accommodated a hundred men.

Set apart from the other barracks were special isolation barracks for disciplinary treatment. These were occupied mostly by the Jehovah's Witnesses, who wore brown triangles and refused to give the Hitler salute or to undergo military service. Often their refusal to abandon their pacifist religious convictions resulted in death.

Historians of the Third Reich may perhaps have exaggerated the extent of the German Churches' 'resistance' to the National Socialist regime, but few have mentioned the martyrdom of the 5,911 Jehovah's Witnesses arrested by the Nazis. More than two thousand perished in concentration camps.

The sinister 'bunker house' for 'hard heads' was isolated from the rest of the inner camp by a wall and a forecourt. Few who vanished into it ever returned alive. Martin Niemöller was locked up in it at this time as 'the Führer's personal prisoner'. The former commander of a submarine which he had scuttled in 1918 rather than surrender to the English, Niemöller had celebrated Hitler's advent as the appearance of God's representative who would 'wield the sword' to avenge the unjust humiliations imposed on Germany by her conquerors. His experience of the Third Reich turned him from a passionate nationalist into an ardent pacifist, and he became one of the presidents of the Ecumenical Council of Churches. When Hitler tried to 'unify' (*gleichschalten*) the Churches, as he had already 'unified' the political parties, the labour unions, schools and the press and information media, Niemöller stood up to him. As a traditional Lutheran, he viewed the authority of the State as inviolable within its own domain but insisted that it stopped short of the Church door. Beyond this was the domain of God and the servants of His word. In the words of the Gospel according to St Matthew (22.21), 'Render unto Caesar that which is Caesar's and unto God that which is God's.'

Unlike the prisoners at Dachau and Buchenwald, healthy Jewish detainees less than sixty years old were put to work with the other prisoners at Sachsenhausen. They dug ditches, or were sent to construction works or the sawmills. It was hard work for most of the men who had never undertaken manual labour. Despite the monotony and the cold in winter, the assignment to the sawmills was the most coveted. The work most feared was at the Hermann Goering brick works, where workers had to gallop with sand and sacks of cement on their shoulders from morning until evening. They paused only at midday, when they were forbidden to sit. Their guards gave them no more rest than a quarter of an hour for a cigarette. Prisoners working with shovels were not allowed to stand up straight, on pain of punishment for an 'infringement of the rules'.

Their heavy routine was envied, however, by the eight to nine hundred 'privileged persons' relieved of work, since these were forced, during their first weeks in detention, to engage in incessant limbering-up exercises on the 'Appelplatz'. Later, exercises were replaced by 'standing to attention', as at Dachau and at Buchenwald. The slightest lapse resulted in the public punishment of the 'guilty party', and sometimes of the whole group, on whom the SS energetically impressed the educational value of these punishments.

The camp commandant was nicknamed 'four corners' because of his small, square build. He never missed an opportunity to stress the 'pedagogical' aims of the system. On the third day after the detainees of 'Operation Crystal Night' arrived, he announced, 'You have been interned here because of your hostile attitude towards our people and our State. This concentration camp is not a prison or a gaol. Neither is it a sanatorium or a rest home. It is a centre for National Socialist education. You must first accustom yourselves to rigid discipline. Punishment will consist of twenty-four blows on the backside to make you hear the music of the spheres, or 'dry hanging', solitary confinement, assignment to a punishment brigade, standing to attention at the main gate of the camp, and so on. In the event that you should contemplate escape, you should know that you will not be shown any mercy: bang – one bullet and the matter is closed. My brave young SS men know how to shoot.'

Turning towards the few Aryan prisoners who had arrived at the same time as the Jews, the commandant added, 'because you are Aryans, our task is to make useful citizens of you, while the Jews need simply to learn how to behave towards their hosts.'

On other occasions the commandant's approach was less 'didactic'. Once, when he ordered a group of prisoners to honour him by turning their heads to the left, he snarled, 'Noses right! I don't want to have to look at your stinking faces.'

He also installed a small private zoo in the camp. He had a row of cages mounted along a wooden wall for his birds, of which he was particularly fond. Above the wall a large notice read, 'Please do not harm them.'

When he was absent, systematic efforts to worry and torture the prisoners in every detail of their daily lives slackened. Supplementary work parties on Sundays were suspended. The men were allowed to sit down in their barracks in the afternoons and even to write. These periods of 'remission' were made use of by the Nazi propagandists, who invited experts to photograph and film scenes which typified the camps' 'exemplary conditions'.

The evening roll-call was obligatory for all prisoners, as was the morning roll-call, but the working prisoners were exempted from the mid-day roll-call. Even the sick and the very young – the 'November arrests' included a number of boys aged between thirteen and sixteen – and the very old, some of whom were over eighty, were all obliged to form ranks. Afterwards they sometimes had 'singing lessons', in which they were required to sing the Sauerland March, or sentimental songs such as 'My Dear Old Mother' or 'The Postillion', or songs composed by some of their comrades. Everyone had to have learned the words in advance, under the supervision of the block leader. Failure to appear or to remember the words warranted the 'regulation' twenty-four blows of the stick.

The midday roll-call was generally for those who had been relieved of work duty. Often rows of old rabbis or semitic-looking 'millionaires' were paraded before journalists and photographers from *Stürmer,* the antisemitic magazine run by the District Party Leader of Nuremberg, or from *Das Schwarze Korps,* the SS publication.

Once, when a prisoner was to be executed for attempting to escape, a rabbi and a pastor were made to carry blasphemous placards to the place of execution.

Food at Sachsenhausen was better than at Dachau or Buchenwald. Breakfast consisted of tapioca pudding and black bread, with a little marmalade on Sundays. Lunch usually consisted of soup, with a bread and margarine 'ration' and some cheese, herrings or pork. After evening roll-call a hot meal of soup, beans, peas or lentils was served. Holidays were the days when inspectors or journalists visited the camp: on such days the prisoners might even be served a good goulash with potatoes.

According to the rules, after he had been in the camp for three weeks an internee was allowed to receive up to fifteen marks a week from his family. With this money he could buy various things to eat at low prices from the canteens. The many prisoners who died at Sachsenhausen, unlike those who perished at the other camps, died less of malnutrition than of physical stress and, with the arrival of winter, of exposure to the cold and damp in inadequate clothing – not to mention deaths caused simply by lack of hygiene.

The life of the Jews at Dachau and Sachsenhausen, however, was comfortable – if one can describe as 'comfortable' conditions which killed a hundred of them and wrecked the lives of most of the survivors – in comparison with the fate of the Jews at Buchenwald. Buchenwald was a stone quarry not far from Weimar, the hub of German culture. In 1938 it housed about 10,000 prisoners, of whom 1,700 were 'common law' detainees, 2,250 Jews rounded up during the summer of 1938, and 300–400 Jehovah's Witnesses, who were particularly helpful to the Jews and even shared their bread rations with them. There were also about 1,000 political prisoners.[8]

One of the political prisoners, Emil Carlebach, had been arrested in 1934 as a young militant communist. He was later to become deputy in the Landtag of Hesse. Thirty years later he recalled the bloodbath with which the SS welcomed the 'November Jews'.[9] His account included the grisly picture of Captain Wolf, a Jewish officer who, during the First World War, had commanded a pursuit squadron in which Marshal Goering had served. When Wolf mentioned that he had been awarded the 'Order of Merit,' the highest German decoration for bravery, the SS responded by crucifying him on the camp's main gate, where he finally died. Carlebach described the Dantesque spectacle of SS troopers, brandishing whips and flanked by police dogs, storming through the barracks and driving nearly seventy of their victims mad in a single night. Then SS Scharführer Martin Sommer smashed in their skulls one by one.

Another of the Buchenwald survivors, the Chief Rabbi of Magdeburg, Dr Georg Wilde, was released after eleven days' detention and emigrated to Great Britain through the intervention of the Chief Rabbi of that country. Dr Wilde has put on record a full account of his experiences after his arrest.[10] 'At about eight in the morning of November 15th,' he recalled, 'after a few days in Magdeburg jail, we were taken to the station. With the single exception of a sneering boy, all of the onlookers around us seemed troubled.'

In other cities, the crowds displayed joy or hatred. In Breslau some women shouted to the SS troopers guarding the prisoners, 'You should have tossed them into the flames when their synagogues were burning.'[11]

They were forbidden to alight during the journey. As the train stopped at different stations Rabbi Wilde flung three postcards from the window of his carriage in the hope of getting in touch with his wife. He hoped that someone would pick them up and post them.

Luckily, one of them actually reached its destination.

'We got off at Weimar, the city of Goethe and Schiller,' Wilde continued.

We were made to hurry down some steps that descended from the platform. In their first exhibition of sadism our new guards had coated these with soap, and the many who slipped were mauled with rifle-butts. Two thousand five hundred members of the Adolf Hitler Guard in grey uniforms continued pummelling us with their rifle-butts all the way to a tunnel. Here we were lined up facing the wall and told, 'Don't turn round. Throw down your knives and razors.'

After we had stood in the darkness for an hour and a half they ordered us to move on. We had to trot over to some armoured trucks which then carried us to the camp. No notice was taken of any who dropped from exhaustion; they stayed where they dropped. Older people had to struggle to hoist themselves into the trucks, which were a good four feet off the ground. The SS lined the running boards and watched us through chinks between the planks. They distracted themselves during the long journey by grabbing prisoners' heads and slamming them to unconsciousness.

Upon our arrival we had to run with hats or skull-caps in hand to a square not far from the main gate. On our way we had to pass between two rows of SS troopers armed with whips, some of which seemed to be fitted with barbed wire or pieces of lead. One trooper, perched on a platform to one side of the gate, swung a great whip down on the heads of passers-by beneath.

One man slumped to the ground at my feet. I managed to side-step him but then lost my footing on the gravel and fell flat on my face. My head was bleeding. I leapt up to hurry on, but an SS trooper was already descending on me. I realized that he was going to hit me in the jaw. More by reflex than by intention I halted in my tracks, so that the blow he landed lost some of its force. He walked away without a word. I was so shocked that I did not feel the pain.

We stood on our feet from morning until evening to be trained in camp 'discipline'. Three men were flogged twenty-five times each as public punishment for some 'infringement' or other. When the victims cried out they received twenty-five more blows. I was too far from them to hear more than the swish of the stick and the yells of the prisoners. I realized that they were trying to unnerve us, to sap our wills and our dignity. An SS officer began screaming, 'None of you will leave this camp alive.' And from that moment I vowed that no matter the cost and no matter how brutal the spectacle I was made to endure, I would not allow my will or my dignity to be belittled. The SS seemed little more than a bunch of maniacs and sadists or the petty henchmen of a criminal gang. I realized that these eighteen-year-old or twenty-three-year-old boys were being systematically trained to display brutality towards everyone in the execution of their orders, whether young or old, innocent or guilty. They were gathering strength for a war against foreign enemies and even against their own people. Whenever I saw the camp commandant I reminded myself that we were civil-ized people, but that he was dirt.

The following morning I saw the corpses of two suicides. One of them had thrown himself against the electrified barbed wire; the other had died from a guard's bullet. The idea of committing suicide never entered my head while I was in detention, even though I was surrounded by large numbers of men who had lost their senses. Later, mental cases were locked in a washroom behind our barracks, and one of my friends, a neurologist, was told to look after them.

The barracks to which the 'November Jews' were assigned were about 250 yards long by eight yards wide and about four yards high. The floors were of beaten turf. The prisoners' bunks consisted of three, or sometimes five, tiers of planks at two-foot intervals. The younger prisoners clambered up to the higher tiers while the eldest occupied the lower ones. Since the prisoners who had arrived earlier had not been able to build four more of these 'temporary barracks' in time to receive the 'November Jews', two to three thousand men were crammed into these hovels like sardines in a tin.

'I thought of a saint who slept on a plank with a log as a pillow,' Rabbi Wilde wrote. 'I concluded that the Nazis wanted to turn us into "super-saints", since we were not given the least suggestion of a pillow.

'Our lives were reduced to extreme simplicity. Without night clothes there was no need to undress in the evening and dress in the morning. There was no need to wash either – this was one of the more painful conditions we lived with – since in our part of the camp there was no water for washing, for the W.C., or for drinking. During the eleven days of my internment not a drop of water touched my skin.'

Another prisoner from Breslau reported that he did not wash once during his eight weeks in the camp. When it rained he eagerly collected in his hat whatever water leaked through the tarred roof of his hut.

'We rose at about half-past three in the morning,' Wilde recounted and lined up in rows of twelve on the parade grounds where the roll was called. Every day, before the counting of prisoners (present or departed), an extraordinarily complicated procedure which lasted several hours, the commandant would look to see if all his 'birds' (his name for the 'November Jews') were still there. Buchenwald (like Sachsenhausen) had its own little zoo, with bull-dogs, eagles, bears, all doted on by the SS and their families.

On good days they gave us a nasty concoction as breakfast coffee. Otherwise our leader, a communist who had been locked up since 1933, would announce, 'I'm sorry but there isn't enough coffee.' He would hand out one cup to ten men and we each sipped a mouthful before passing the cup on to the next. On really bad days we got none at all and had to wait until soup was served. First a group of Jewish prisoners dragged away the night's crop, the six or seven corpses. They were left at the camp gate to be carted off to a crematorium at Weimar or Jena. In those days families could still claim the cinders.

Since the 'November Jews' were not detailed to work duty like 'ordinary' prisoners, they sometimes waited for their soup from midday until evening, and sometimes in vain. Dr Wilde gladly gave his share to hungrier fellow-prisoners. His throat was so parched that it was painful to swallow the soup, which was normally very salty. But there was nothing else with which to wash down the bread ration. He was constantly thirsty. He dreamt of water, tea, coffee.

One night, it must have been about two o'clock, one of my former pupils came to tell me that a man near the door had a bottle of coffee and was distributing a spoonful per person. I got up and received my spoonful of coffee as if it were a spoonful of medicine. I rinsed my mouth several times with this single mouthful before swallowing it drop by drop. Ever since that night I have kept a glass of tea within reach on my bedside table so as to remind myself that I can drink if I need to.

The camp had a canteen, of course. But we were not allowed to buy anything during the first few days. Later, two or three men were assigned to fetch orders for the others. Given our numbers and the relative 'brevity' of my detention, my only purchases were a bottle of mineral water and a small tin of biscuits, which I shared with the members of my congregation who had no money. The predicament of the orthodox Jews was particularly moving. Despite the circumstances, they stubbornly refused hot food because it was not kosher and lived on dry bread, 'coffee' and herbal teas.

During my stay in the camp I never once sat down on a chair.

We were on our feet all day. This was all the more difficult for the older persons since our shoes were worn out by the muddy walks we were forced to take. One morning I fainted. My neighbour spread me out on the ground, put something on my head and covered me with a coat. I don't know how long I was unconscious, but when I came round and realized what had happened I decided to stay as I was for as long as possible. I shut my eyes, and the passing guards noticed nothing but a pallid old man with a white beard stretched out unconscious on the ground. They probably assumed I was dead and walked straight past. Although it meant sacrificing my coffee I was glad not to have to stand up.

As a sadistic alternative to standing roll-call there were 'sitting days', when we were made to sit down on the gravel. Anyone who stood up to go to the toilet was given ten, fifteen or twenty lashes. If he yelled he was strung up on the window-grill of the administrative block with hands bound behind his back, in such a way that his toes just reached the ground. Later he disappeared for ever to the 'bunker'.

Getting up during these 'sitting' days amounted to incurring the death penalty.[12]

As it was a dry sunny day I decided to get up for soup. Perhaps I was so exhausted because the previous night had been unusually disrupted. Two men had gone mad in our barracks. After they had been taken away we could still hear their screams while they were beaten until they shut up. Then a man in my congregation went mad. One of my former pupils suggested that he bring him to me. 'Perhaps you can calm him down.' A wisp of a man came. He stared into my eyes and kept mumbling, 'Tomorrow they are going to kill me and you, too.'

'That's right,' I answered. 'But until then why don't you lie down here beside me? There's room for you. Lie down. We can rest for two or three hours. How can we deal with what is in store if we are not well rested?'

This seemed to convince him and he lay down beside me. A few weeks later, when I saw him again, he seemed to have recovered. A converted Jew walked round, making the sign of the cross and shouting, 'Jesus said I am love'.

In hut IA an old Jew, who had owned a large business in Silesia, went mad when he was forced to sell it. Night and day he explained the various phases of the sale, the valuation of his merchandise, the prices fixed by the Nazis. It had all been settled, but he still worried about what had happened to his employees. That, he said, would also be taken care of. He was telling his story for the tenth time when a drunken SS trooper stumbled into the hut. The old businessman thought he had come for an explanation and tried to justify himself. 'Herr Schaufürer, be assured that I shall take care of my employees.'

The trooper tried to shove the old man away, but he continued his story inexorably.

Wild with rage, the trooper grabbed his arm and dragged him from the barracks. Two shots crashed through the night and settled the old man's affairs.[13] As a precaution the members of the Union of Jewish Veterans of the Reich, with younger men under their command, organized a night guard to sound the alarm whenever the SS approached and to maintain order inside the barracks.

Madness became an increasingly frequent event owing to idleness, ill-treatment, and the unhygienic conditions in which the 'November Jews' were forced to live at Buchenwald. Some died of dysentery or drowned in the latrines, which consisted of simple pits over which large wooden beams had been laid. Since medicine was not available the prisoners pooled four hundred marks of their own money to buy some. The camp officers, however, objected. Jewish doctors, they claimed, were surely capable enough to cure their fellow Jews without the aid of medicine. A Jewish doctor from Breslau went mad at the sight of fellow-prisoners seriously ill in their bunks without medicine.

'We recognize only two kinds of people here,' Commandant Koch announced at one of the roll-calls, 'the healthy, and the sick, who are sent to the crematorium.'[14]

In context, the Commandant's statement merely confirmed to the prisoners that they had no choice but to accept their fate or die. Their cadavers would be sent for incineration in the municipal crematoriums at Weimar and Jena. Apart from being a sinister threat, the Commandant's formula revealed the torturer's state of mind long before the 'final solution' began to be applied.

Conversation among the 'November Jews' revolved around a single topic: their eventual release. Some of them thought that an emigration visa – that is, an undertaking to quit Germany for ever – would be sufficient to obtain freedom. This idea had occurred to Rabbi Wilde before he arrived at the camp, while his group of prisoners were on their way to Magdeburg station. He had shouted to a Gestapo officer whom he knew, 'Please tell Herr H. [who was in charge of Jewish emigration] to get my papers ready.'

The officer nodded.

'But another Gestapo officer who was escorting us said, "There's no point. You'll be released in a week anyway."

'When the week was nearly up and we were still in the camp, a rumour circulated that men over sixty would be released. The next day we were assembled to be released.'

If Müller's and Heydrich's instructions had, in fact, been followed, men over sixty would not have been arrested in the first place.

'One of my congregation begged me to leave him my handkerchief.

' "But it's torn."

' "It doesn't matter. It's better than no handkerchief at all. I can't thank you enough."

'In the absence of the SS, an Australian Jew recorded our identities in one of the administrative offices. It took hours. Then we returned to our groups and heard nothing more. I felt let down. The weather was turning colder. A glacial wind rose. I put on all the underclothing I had with me and one of my pupils had lent me an extra undershirt. But I knew that I would not survive eternal hours of standing in the rain and sleeping in wet clothing.'

The 'November Jews' at Buchenwald were allowed to keep their clothing unless they were between twenty and forty years old.

On the eleventh day of internment the loudspeakers suddenly announced, 'Attention, all you Jews. I shall now read the names of those who will be released today.'

The tension was unbearable. I was so exhausted I didn't hear my name. One of my congregation ran up, shouting happily, 'Georg Wilde, born May 9th 1877, free.'

There must have been about two hundred of us. In fact our numbers shrank to 194 because six died between the announcement and their departure. We were led into a room for a 'medical examination'. I immediately realized that the only purpose of this examination was to see if any scars were left from the brutal treatment we had received. Men whose sores were too obvious were not released. When the doctor noticed the scar on my cranium from the fall that occurred when I arrived, he asked, 'Does it still hurt?'

When I replied that it didn't, I was allowed to go on. Rabbi Ochs from Gleiwitz, who had been horribly beaten by the SS when we arrived, was given ultra-violet treatment to make his sores heal faster.

We were then ordered to go to the barber. The rules then in force in German prisons and camps required prisoners' heads and faces to be shaven. When we arrived at the camp Jewish barbers were supposed to shave and clip us, but they had worked long into the night without completing their work. The following day more prisoners arrived, and in the confusion of those first days we were forgotten. I was glad to escape this annoying regulation when we arrived and decided to do all I could to elude it as I left. This was why I asked the communist prisoner who was in charge of us to request authorization from the SS Oberscharführer for me to keep my hair and especially my beard.

'Why do you want to keep it?'

'I am a Rabbi and it is customary for Rabbis to wear beards.'

He looked frightened and I realized that he would not dare to do as I asked. Summoning up my courage, I approached the SS officer directly, making an attempt at a show of military bearing by clicking my heels. Respect for military traditions in Germany always helped to ease relations.

'Herr Oberscharführer, may I request permission to keep my hair, especially my beard?'

'Why?'

I repeated my explanation.

'I haven't the authority to decide. Ask the other section commander.'

The same question received the same reply.

I didn't realize that I was performing the *Taming of the Shrew* a dangerous game under such circumstances. The SS officer was so amazed that he ordered the barber to leave my beard.

'I'm very sorry, Herr Oberscharführer,' the barber replied. 'My orders are to shave and cut everyone. If I don't, I'll get twenty-five blows of the stick.'

'In that case, shave me. I don't want to be responsible for that.'

But one of the Nazis suggested that we call the Camp Commandant on the telephone.

'You are the Chief Rabbi, aren't you?' one of the SS officers asked, as if trying to help by reminding me of my title.

All the Camp Commandant's orders issued from the loudspeaker system. Two minutes later the twenty thousand prisoners at Buchenwald listened in amazement to the 'Judgment of Solomon' from the Kommandatur. 'By order of the Commandant, the Jew and Chief Rabbi Dr Wilde is authorized to keep his beard. His head will be shaven.'

A moment later an SS officer, a real brute, rushed in shouting, 'Where is the Chief Rabbi?'

When he caught sight of me he smiled like an old friend. Another SS officer courteously asked me if I was the Chief Rabbi. Instead of simply saying 'yes', I said 'Jawohl,' the affirmative used when speaking to officers of the German Army. I wondered if he grasped the significance of my reply, the only one I could use in this sinister comedy. Although in other circumstances he would certainly have tortured me to death for such insolence, he silently acquiesced like a beaten dog. The Commandant's little favour, possibly a drunkard's whim, had transformed these animals into servile lap-dogs.

We paraded through the main gate of the camp at five in the evening. Above it on the outside was written 'JUST OR UNJUST THIS IS MY FATHERLAND,' and on the inside cut-out letters in the grill read 'EACH HIS DUTY'.

I thought we had been released, but we were being taken to the political section office. Again we had to wait hours on our feet in a narrow corridor. My neighbour fainted. He died in the train not far from his home village.

A high-ranking Gestapo officer finally emerged from his office. 'If any of you do not hear well,' he said, 'will you please move closer.'

'There is one deaf-mute here,' someone answered.

'We are allowing you to return home so that you may make the necessary arrangements to emigrate. If you say one word about the concentration camp, however, we shall bring you back and you will never leave again. Don't think you can get away with saying what you like outside Germany. We have agents everywhere in the world and they will shut you up for ever.'

After this unambiguous pronouncement we each signed a declaration that we had no complaints, that we had been treated fairly and that we understood that we were to tell no one of our experience. Our civilian clothing was then returned with the possessions we had surrendered on arrival and we were released with a caution not to get drunk.

Our group marched to the nearest village, where we found bread, cheese, mineral water and coffee to satisfy hunger and thirst. The innkeeper seemed to understand as we approached what people arriving from the 'hill' needed. (The camp at Buchenwald was on the hill of Ettersberg.) He was friendly and asked no questions about the camp. Three old peasants sat silently drinking their beer at a nearby table.

Five hours later Rabbi Wilde rejoined his wife at Magdeburg. The following morning he was ordered to report to local Gestapo headquarters to sign an undertaking that he would voluntarily emigrate before April 15th 1939. Less fortunate were the thousands of other prisoners detained after 'Crystal Night' who waited weeks, often months, for replies to desperate requests for emigration visas. They would go anywhere to escape the hell of the camps. Through friends or relatives many managed to buy false emigration permits, which some Latin American consulates sold for several hundred marks.

Until they were released, every screw was turned to wring the last penny from the Jewish prisoners so as to fill the pockets of their tormentors. Herman Striem from Breslau, who lost thirty-five pounds during his eight weeks' detention at Buchenwald, recalled that two weeks after his arrival he and his fellow prisoners were ordered to 'write postcards to your families telling them that you have arrived safely, that you are well, but that you need underclothing, warm clothing, good shoes and woollen blankets.'

Hundreds of packages soon streamed in, but they rarely reached their destinations. The SS tried to convince prisoners that these packages were more urgently needed by the National Socialist Winter Aid. On another occasion, after the prisoners had witnessed an execution, the camp authorities announced that Jews who possessed cars would immediately be released if they surrendered their ownership of them. Shaken by the grisly spectacle, several hundred rushed forward to make their 'donations'. They were not, however, released. A more sordid procedure was involved in requests to families of 'November Jews' to send money to pay for purchases from the canteen. When the money arrived SS troopers at one table handed the letters over while troopers at a second table confiscated any sums that exceeded ten marks.

The first 'November Jews' to be released left Sachsenhausen after six days' internment. Those at Dachau and Buchenwald followed a few days later. Men over sixty, the seriously ill, those who could certify their intention to emigrate or who agreed to sell their businesses to Aryans for laughable sums were permitted to leave. Loudspeakers daily gave the order for Jews who owned cars, houses or other movable or immovable property to report to the authorities. The 'final solution' had not yet been adopted at this time. No one was yet being sent to the gas-chambers. But the terror which the 'November Jews' were daily made to endure was calculated to make them emigrate at any cost, even if it meant leaving behind all they possessed.

The release of prisoners was staggered over several months between November 18th 1938 and the Spring of 1939. The cold, the ill-treatment and the typhus epidemic caused by the lack of any hygienic facilities in the Jewish barracks at Dachau and Buchenwald claimed the lives of hundreds of people whose names belong on the roll of victims from the 'Crystal Night'. According to the most modest estimates, based on documents at the Wiener Library, the pogrom claimed the lives of between 2,000 and 2,500 men, women and children, and permanently affected all the others who survived its horror.

6

The Nations That Looked On

It is worth considering the way in which the outside world responded to these pogroms. The fascist or authoritarian regimes in Italy, Rumania, Hungary and Poland were the only governments who approved. They took the pogroms as a case to stiffen their own policies, particularly by reinforcing antisemitic legislation. Nationalist groups in Poland even issued a statement that brutal measures offered the only hope of getting rid of the Jews on an international scale.[1]

Most other countries were indignant. But within the context of international relations weak countries, dependent on the great powers for protection, could do little. The Latin American governments looked to Washington, but wished to safeguard good relations with all European countries, including Germany. The British colonies waited to hear His Majesty's government's reactions, while the French Empire probed the situation in Paris.

In the case of some European countries, such as Greece, pressure was exerted by Nazi Germany. On the day after the 'Crystal Night' the Greek press published reports from the press agencies Reuter and Havas, but then the Government in Athens was directed not to publish further reports on the events unless they emanated from official German sources.[2] Metaxas' police quietly co-operated with the action taken by the German Ambassador to Athens. After the Ambassador had summoned the Germans resident in Greece to declare which of them were not of Aryan extraction, the Greek police reassembled them to confirm the reckoning and to cancel residence permits. The Germans took no further action; the Greek police renewed the residence permits, but then closed Greece's frontiers to Jewish refugees from Germany and Italy. The Jews who were most severely affected were those, chiefly Greco-Spanish, in the large congregation· in Salonica. For German firms now closed their agencies, of which the Jews in Salonica had previously had nearly exclusive control in Greece.

Salazar's Portugal adopted a more equivocal attitude. Except for the fascist newspaper *Diario da Manha,* the press condemned the anti-Jewish measures as a lapse from moral standards. In an article entitled 'Punishment without Crime' the Lisbon newspaper *Diario de Noticias* declared:

> We feel that nothing can excuse these brutal events, even if we take into account the limited credibility to which the press in Paris, London and New York are entitled in view of their dedication to the Israelite cause and their constant attempts to incite war against all nationalism, to the detriment of Israel.
>
> Thousands have paid for a crime which they did not commit, for no other reason than that they are Jews. . . .
>
> . . . We speak in the name of a legal conscience which is alarmed by the shameful contempt in which human rights are held. We speak in the name of civilization, which has been robbed of moral standards if a Jew's life on the scales of justice and in the estimation of the Aryans is not worth as much as any other. We endorse a doctrine of social order in which the policies of governments are influenced by morality and neither assassination nor plunder can ever be counted among the actions or reactions of a ruling authority.[3]

Among the smaller European democracies, Holland expressed the keenest sympathy with the victims. The Dutch press unanimously deplored the pogrom. The lower house of the government met to debate the refugee problem and to work out a suspension of immigration restrictions so that the victims could be admitted. A large number of committees were spontaneously formed throughout the little country to offer assistance to refugees. More than a million florins were collected in a few days. Some cities readily offered to co-operate by receiving Jewish children, while the government ordered the construction of two reception centres. The Dutch fully expected some form of international co-operation to be undertaken, since their means were too limited to enable them to bear the full brunt of the refugee problem for long.

This anxiety was even more sharply felt in the Scandinavian countries. The Danish and Swedish press were unanimously sympathetic with the victims of persecution. The Nazi action, they felt, had undermined the chance of extending the Munich policies. But they were also concerned about the fate of the 500,000–600,000 Jews to whom not even a modest refuge had been offered. 'Europe is inundated with refugees, but there must certainly be a place for them elsewhere in the world.'[4]

Public opinion in Sweden betrayed yet greater reservations on this point. 'No matter how great the sympathy for the Jews may be in Sweden,' the American Ambassador to Sweden noted, 'it is apparent that no one really wants to take the risk of creating a Jewish problem in Sweden also by a liberal admission of Jewish refugees.'[5] This attitude was shared by the Jewish minority in Sweden, who were apprehensive that an influx of Jewish refugees might arouse antisemitic sentiments. They raised funds to help their fellow Jews in Germany to emigrate to countries outside Europe.

The Swiss authorities were moved by the same fear of being overrun. In March 1938 they had persuaded the Nazis authorities to stamp a distinctive J in passports issued to German and Austrian Jews (see page 23). On November 11th, the day after the 'Crystal Night', they promptly ratified a German–Swiss agreement, one of whose provisions was as follows: 'The agencies of the German government concerned with passport control and guarding the German–Swiss frontier shall be instructed to prevent the entry into Switzerland of any German Jew or any Jew whose passport does not bear a residence or transit permit issued by the Swiss government.

142

THE NATIONS THAT LOOKED ON

'The German government, in accord with the government of Switzerland, also reserves the right to require Jews of Swiss nationality to obtain a residence or transit permit before entering German territory.'

Although the reciprocal clause aroused some indignation in Swiss public opinion, there was no protest against the first part of the agreement, which the majority of Latin American nations hurriedly copied. It is significant, furthermore, that a former police officer at Saint Gall, Paul Grueninger, waited thirty-one years before the Swiss government recognized an impressive number of appeals on his behalf by people whose lives he had saved and revoked the 'dismissal without compensation' imposed when he was found 'guilty of permitting Jews fleeing Nazism to enter Swiss territory without visas and of furnishing false papers in order to protect them from expulsion.'⁶ Edgar Bonjour, a Swiss historian, confirmed in a report on Swiss neutrality that 'the self-centred, latent antisemitism which every citizen harboured made him ignore the inhumanity embodied in some aspects of the official policy on the right to asylum.'

It is difficult, however, to condemn the small nations when one considers the example set by the large ones.

Article 129 of the constitution of the powerful Union of Soviet Socialist Republics provided for granting asylum to victims of political persecution. Soviet Russia had admitted a small number of refugees, mostly communists fleeing from the advent of Nazism, from the Spanish Civil War or from the Austrian Anschluss. But it adopted a dilatory attitude towards Jewish refugees. The Soviet press did report on the antisemitic persecutions. In a leading article in *Pravda* of November 16th 1938, the editor compared the German pogrom with the pogroms in Tsarist Russia and took it as a symptom of the German fascists' weakness. 'The economic difficulties and the discontent of the masses,' he wrote under the name of 'Observer', 'have forced the fascist leaders to resort to a pogrom against the Jews to distract the attention of the masses from grave problems within the country. . . . But antisemitic pogroms did not save the Tsarist monarchy, and they will not save German fascism from destruction.'

The next day another editorial in *Pravda,* couched in a more graphic style, reached the same conclusions: 'This latest orgy of cannibalistic pogroms is a sign that the end of fascism is near.' With satisfaction and concern this second editorial also emphasized the shock with which the Anglo-Saxons had reacted to Nazi terror, since they had previously favoured a policy of appeasement towards the Third Reich. A report on the paper's front page described the indignant reactions of the international press, reminding its readers that the bourgeoisie had always refused to recognize what the workers of the world had seen as obvious: that antisemitic pogroms were not an isolated episode in fascist countries but a deliberate expression of the same policies which the fascists adopted at home and in international affairs.

But the Soviet newspapers withheld until November 27th, two weeks after the 'Crystal Night', any mention of the public protests held in the large cities throughout Soviet Russia. At these protest meetings, Soviet intellectuals denounced 'fascist savagery' and contrasted the racial persecution in Germany and Italy with the equality of rights conferred on all citizens of the USSR. No mention was made in these reports of any concrete attempt by the USSR to deal with the problem of Jewish refugees. It is significant that no official from the government or the Communist Party spoke at any of these meetings, and still more significant that Ivan Papanin, head of a scientific expedition to the North Pole and a member of the Supreme Soviet, declared in an interview with an American journalist that he was in favour of the admission of German Jewish refugees and thought that the next session of the Supreme Soviet might discuss the matter. In accordance with the prevailing rules the text of the interview was submitted to the Soviet authorities for approval. The version which the American was authorized to publish contained no allusion to the problem of Jewish refugees.[7]

The only clue to official policies that we have was contained in a letter in which Ivan Maiski, the Soviet Ambassador to London, replied on December 2nd 1938 to an inquiry from Sir Neill Malcolm,

League of Nations High Commissioner for German and Austrian refugees:

> On November 2nd you asked if the Soviet government was disposed to receive a certain number of refugees currently under your protection as High Commissioners of the League of Nations for German refugees. These persons have been forced, as a result of Nazi persecutions, to leave their countries and seek temporary asylum in Czechoslavakia, France, Belgium, etc. You indicated that about nine-tenths of them are Jewish and that their living conditions are exceedingly precarious. In order to relieve their suffering you proposed that the Union of Soviet Socialist Republics should admit a certain number of them into its territory, particularly those in the following categories:

> (a) highly qualified specialists such as engineers, doctors, agronomists, etc.
> (b) persons qualified in agriculture.

> As I mentioned at the time of our meeting, although I was not then able immediately to reply, I promised to submit your request to my government.

> I am now able to forward to you the Soviet Government's reply. My government states that it is willing in principle to receive a certain number of refugees within the categories specified above, but that a decision will be taken in respect of each individual case.[8]

Needless to say, this 'decision in principle' was never actually put into practice. Soviet Russia under Stalin, which was then in the throes of its own internal purges, did not so much as consider being burdened with foreign elements, least of all with Jews. As early as 1934 Helena Strassova, Secretary General of the International Red Cross, affirmed that the official Soviet policy, even in so far as internal problems were concerned, consisted in 'urging the capitalist countries to grant refugees asylum,' rather than in accepting them into the USSR.

The Attitude of the Three Great Western Powers

Of the three great western powers – Great Britain, France and the United States – Great Britain, or British public opinion, undoubtedly responded most vigorously after the 'Crystal Night.' This episode was felt to be a brutal betrayal of Prime Minister Chamberlain's policy of appeasement towards the Third Reich. Despite Hitler's venomous attacks on Churchill's political supporters, however, and despite statements in the German press that went so far as to name Churchill, Attlee, and Duff Cooper as 'instigators of the Jewish assassination,'[9] British diplomats tried to resist pressure to upset Anglo-German understanding.

Dr Weizmann, Executive Chairman of the Jewish Agency, had received warnings from Jewish congregations in Germany on November 9th and requested the Foreign Office to appoint a prominent non-Jew to approach the Nazi leaders immediately. When the British Ambassador to Germany, Sir Nevile Henderson (who was in London at the time), was consulted by the Foreign Minister, Lord Halifax, he replied that he saw no advantage in such a procedure and, indeed, only disadvantages.[10] (Five days later the British Ambassador was to confirm his American counterpart's agreement that their intervention would do more harm than good.)

When the pogrom was imminent the Jewish congregation in Berlin approached Sir Michael Bruce, a retired British diplomat who, at the request of the Chief Rabbi of Great Britain, had travelled to Germany with the intention of interceding with the Nazis on behalf of the Jewish population. Bruce first gathered information about the forthcoming pogrom. Then, he recalled, 'I went at once to the British Embassy. I told Sir George Ogilvie-Forbes everything I knew and urged him to contact Hitler and express Britain's displeasure. He told me he could do nothing. The Ambassador Sir Nevile Henderson, was in London and the Foreign Office, acting on instructions from Lord Halifax, had told him to do nothing that might offend Hitler and his minions.'[11]

British public opinion, the press and even some prominent figures who had until then advocated Anglo-German understanding exhibited their indignation with great vigour. The Archbishop of Canterbury, Cosmo Gordon Lang, who had been one of the heartiest supporters of friendship with the new Germany, felt obliged to express the disapproval of the Christians of the United Kingdom in a letter to the *Times* of November 12th: 'Whatever provocation may have been given by the deplorable act of a single irresponsible Jewish youth, reprisals on such a scale, so fierce, cruel and vindictive, cannot possibly be justified. A sinister significance is added to them by the fact that the police seem either to have acquiesced in them or to have been powerless to restrain them. It is most distasteful to write these words just when there is in this country a general desire to be on friendly terms with the German nation. But there are times when the mere instincts of humanity make silence impossible. Would that the rulers of the Reich could realize that such excesses of hatred and malice put upon the friendship which we are ready to offer them an almost intolerable strain.' The Archbishop concluded by calling upon the Churches of the United Kingdom to pray for the victims of persecution 'whose future seems to be so dark and hopeless'.

In this heated atmosphere Lord Mount Temple, President of the Anglo-German Society, resigned on the grounds that he would not abide either the treatment meted out to the Jews nor the hostile attitude of the German government towards Catholics and Protestants in Germany.

A Gallup Poll asked, 'Do you think the persecution of German Jews is an obstacle to good relations between Great Britain and Germany?' Four out of five who replied said 'yes'.

The German ambassador to London described to his government[12] with some concern the negative reaction which anti-Jewish measures had provoked and the ensuing wave of anti-German feeling in Great Britain. He blamed, mainly, the attitude of the British press and Jewish influence on British leaders. He was most troubled by the pessimism felt by Englishmen who favoured an Anglo-German rapprochement and by the weakening of Chamberlain's position.

The press reflected the reluctance with which public opinion in Britain had embraced the policy of appeasement. 'There is no war party in this country,' wrote the political commentator 'Scrutator', 'but I fancy that before long we shall have a Government that will stand for a strong democratic Britain, that, in turn, will stand for freedom and justice the world over and will face even war rather than forswear the right, abandon the weak and suffer the threats, insults, and aggressions of criminal-minded upstarts.'[13]

In Parliament an important debate was held on religious, political and 'racial minorities'. Sir Philip Noel-Baker, the Labour Member of Parliament for Derby and later awarded the Nobel Peace Prize, vigorously and courageously pleaded the cause of the Jewish victims.[14] He described the terror which had been unleashed on the Jews in Germany simply because of their origin and recalled their contributions to a country which had cradled Protestantism and Kant, a great labour movement and a great tradition of freedom of the press. He reminded the House of Commons of Goebbels' menacing words after the pogroms: 'We only want the world to be sufficiently pro-Jewish to take all our Jews from our shoulders.'[15]

The threat of expulsion which hounded the Jews in Germany also extended to the Jews in Hungary, Rumania and Poland, since these countries were eager to follow Hitler's example. Noel-Baker proposed a two-point programme: the threat of reprisals, if need be, to halt the arrest and expulsion of penniless victims; and the immediate creation of a rehabilitation agency for the hundreds of thousands of emigrants. He recalled that the League of Nations had dealt with a considerably larger number of displaced persons after the First World War. What was needed was concerted international effort and money.

'If the government can guarantee a loan for arms to Turkey,' Noel-Baker said, 'I think they ought to guarantee a loan to save these unhappy people.' He had no illusions about the good-will of Chamberlain's government, and felt it necessary to add that 'the power of vigilant and instructed opinion will break these obstructions down.' He closed with an appeal to the conscience of the government and of humanity. 'I think they [the Government] might in some measure stay the tyrant's hand in Germany by the means I have suggested. Certainly they can gather the resources, human and material, that are needed to make a new life for this pitiful human wreckage. That wreckage is the result of the mistakes made by all the Governments during the last twenty years. Let the Governments now atone for those mistakes. The refugees have surely endured enough. Dr Goebbels said the other day that he hoped the outside world would soon forget the German Jews. He hopes in vain. His campaign against them will go down in history with St Bartholomew's Eve as a lasting memory of human shame. Let there go with it another memory, the memory of what the other nations did to wipe the shame away.'

It was a vain hope. Contrary to the anxieties of the German Ambassador to London, neither the outrage which the British felt nor a debate in the House of Commons induced Chamberlain to reverse his policy of concessions to Hitler. One such concession was the restitution of former German colonies. Chamberlain asked Oswald Pirow,[16] the South African Minister of Defence, Industry and Commerce, to explain to Hitler, who received him at Berchtesgaden on November 24th, what disastrous effects his antisemitic policies could have on British friendship. Pirow, the son of a nineteenth-century German émigré, warmly admired Hitler's regime. He explained to Hitler that if he turned his back on Great Britain the war party there would gain ascendance and a terrible world-wide conflict would ensue. Hitler should rather sustain Chamberlain and Halifax as men of good-will in their struggle against the war party which was being marshalled by Churchill and Duff Cooper. He should co-operate with England and the United States to finance Jewish emigration.

Hitler saw red. The Jews, he said, would one day vanish from the face of Europe. Many other countries were troubled by the activities of the Jews within their frontiers. As far as he was concerned he would not be responsible for handing over to the Jews the last vestiges of foreign reserves still in German hands.

Pirow launched into a long-winded explanation. He requested

among other things that the Führer help other countries to finance emigration by exchanging merchandise and, what would certainly be more attractive, by offering one of the former German colonies (Tanganyika, for example) as a base for Jewish emigration. Pirow hoped at the same time to rescue South West Africa from the claims of German greed. He felt his suggestion would create a new and more favourable context within which to discuss the colonial problem. But Hitler indignantly refused. How could he abandon the lands for which so many German heroes had shed their blood? He could not simply hand them over to Germany's most resolute enemies.[17]

Pirow's mission to Hitler was completely abortive. He fared no better with Mussolini. When Pirow asked him to act as mediator, Mussolini showed him the door, cursing 'the rapidity with which a race living in another latitude could deteriorate. It was almost impossible to believe that Pirow's father had been a German. Pirow was quite right when he always described himself as an African.'[18]

While Pirow was meeting Hitler at Berchtesgaden in his effort to convince him that there could be an African solution to the Jewish problem, Chamberlain discussed the problem with Daladier in a series of Franco-British talks which preceded Ribbentrop's visit to Paris. The Chamberlain–Daladier meeting, held at the Quai d'Orsay,[19] was attended by the British and French foreign ministers, Lord Halifax and Georges Bonnet. Bonnet voiced the French government's anxieties. A certain number of Jewish refugees had recently been admitted, even though France already had forty thousand. According to Bonnet the French government would admit a few more and would consider settling some others in French colonies, provided, however, that Great Britain and the United States made similar efforts.

Chamberlain accepted the challenge: 'Mr Chamberlain said that His Majesty's Government were most anxious to help; and that they had already taken this matter up with the Colonies and Dominions,' state the minutes of the meeting. 'One of the chief difficulties, however, was the serious danger of arousing antisemitic feeling in Great Britain. Indeed, a number of Jews had begged His Majesty's Gov-

ernment not to advertise too prominently what was being done.'
For the information of the French government, Chamberlain added,
Britain was weekly admitting five hundred Jewish refugees. He
omitted to say that public opinion had forced him to take this
measure. As far as the Empire was concerned, the Australians were
admitting a significant number; but they dealt with each case individually and without publicity for the reasons already stated. The
proposal to settle Jews in Tanganyika had been favourably received
by that country but had been rejected by the German government,
which argued that Tanganyika was legally a German colony and
should, in due course, revert to Germany. According to Chamberlain, there were alternatives, such as Northern Rhodesia, Kenya or
British Guiana, but the Jewish organizations would have to finance a
colonization programme. The British Prime Minister did not expect
assistance from the American government but he hoped that American Jews would contribute. For the moment it was essential for the
German government to authorize Jewish émigrés to take property
away with them. Chamberlain did not conceal his hope that the
French government would exert its influence to this end on the
German Foreign Minister during his visit to Paris.

This visit (combined with the hope that a deepening of Franco-
German understanding, along the lines of the Munich agreement,
would be achieved) played a decisive part in subduing the French
government's reactions to the 'Crystal Night' and, by its influence,
those of the press as well.

The newspapers of the extreme right naturally seized the opportunity to recite their favoured antisemitic and xenophobic slogans.
An example can be quoted from *Action Française*:

A crime which may provoke the gravest consequences was
committed yesterday at the German Embassy in Paris. Once again
its author was a foreigner, a Polish Jew.
Will France always serve as a battleground for every foreign
pig in Europe and in the world? Must we always bear the brunt
of perfidious acts such as that committed yesterday?

France is a hospitable country. It will not allow a properly accredited diplomat to be assassinated in Paris by a foreign pig who was evading a deportation order.

Why was the order not carried out? That is the key question. We wonder how many other foreigners are living among us under the same irregular circumstances as Grynszpan Herschel Feibel.

On October 14th our excellent and courageous friend Charles Trochu submitted a written question to the Prefect of the Seine and the Prefect of Police demanding that they stem the invasion of 'foreign refugees, particularly Jews expelled from Germany and Italy.

'The interests of national defence and of the economy do not permit us to support the foreign elements which have recently installed themselves in and around our capital.

'Paris has too long been a dumping ground for international hoodlums, the right of asylum must have limits. . . .'

After three weeks Charles Trochu, whose argument has acquired fresh support from last night's events, has still failed to receive a reply. . . .[20]

A significant fact was noted by the American chargé d'affaires in Paris. The moderate press, including *Figaro* and Emile Roche's radical socialist *République* as well as *Le Temps,* the ancestor of *Le Monde,* merely reported the events of the 'Crystal Night' without suggesting how they might affect French policy.[21]

The House of Commons debated the event, but the French National Assembly was silent. An editorial in *Le Temps* of November 16th on the 'Jewish Problem' conceded that 'one cannot honestly allow an entire race to drift towards suicide and extinction simply because unrestrained political passions hurl the most terrible humiliations down on them.' It was regrettable that 'the persecution of the Jews in Germany and the reactions which it has aroused, particularly in the Anglo-Saxon nations, portended an atmosphere unfavourable to a policy of understanding and co-operation such as might confidently have been expected after the Munich Agreements.'

Some leader-writers were disconcerted by this ambiguous political attitude. Emile Buré summed up in *L'Ordre:* 'I would not recommend an ideological crusade, but we should take care that in wilfully ignoring the sufferings of minorities subject to Nazi laws, and in appeasing those who decree them and apply them, often with deliberate sadism, France and England may through indifference and complacency bring upon themselves the same evils which already afflict the individuals and groups which have asked them to intercede. At all events, their misguided policies are quickly sapping away what little prestige remains to them.'[22]

The left-wing weekly *La Lumière* was blunter. In an article entitled 'What Barbarity! The World is Outraged! France is Silent,'[23] Albert Bayet condemned the fear and indifference which dominated French politics. 'In the past, when we protested against massacres in Ethiopia, China, Spain, we were told, "Silence! You are warmongering." When we protested against the mutilation of Czechoslovakia we were told, "Keep quiet! You are a war party." Today, when we protest against the contemptible persecution of defenceless Jews and their wives and their children, we are told, "Be silent! France is afraid".'

There was some cause for indignation when a French publication which called itself left-wing and whose political opinions were guided by a Jew, Albert Milhaud, dared to suggest that France, the country of the rights of man, should impose a quota on Jewish immigration.

'I am deeply offended as a human being and as a Frenchman,' Albert Bayet added, 'that while the American, British, and Dutch governments spoke up, our government said nothing. . . .

'Compounded with all our other omissions, silence amounts to approval. If France were to keep silent it would cease to be France. I am certain that this will not happen. It cannot happen. The hour of awakening is near. May our country not be judged by its venial press which dishonours it nor by the official silences which betray it.'

The Socialist Party (SFIO) expressed the same disapproval of the government's attitude. Its official journal published a resolution of its executive committee 'noting with regret that of all the governments of the democratic countries only the French ministers had not thought fit to express publicly their disapproval of the Nazis government's crimes, which had been branded by statesmen such as President Roosevelt and the British Prime Minister Neville Chamberlain. The SFIO urges workers to combine forces before the hateful repression embodied in fascism, and to join with the Socialist party in opposing all racial prejudice and in defending the conquests of democracy and the rights of man against adversaries.'[24]

At the time that opposition to Hitler's regime was being mobilized, the LICA (International League Against Antisemitism) and its magazine *Le Droit de Vivre,* edited by Bernard Lecache, called upon Christians, Jews, Muslims and Free-thinkers to attend a rally at the Mutualité.

Such open and humane sentiments, however, did not sway the supporters of the Munich policy. A left-wing historian might expect the debate to reflect the traditional division between the Right and the Left. But we have already examined the attitude of some Radical Socialists. To these we must add a significant sector of the Jewish middle-classes in Sweden, Great Britain, France and the United States, who feared that an influx of Jewish refugees would lead to antisemitism at home and war with Germany abroad. It was in the light of this preoccupation that the noted and respected Chief Rabbi of Paris, Julien Weill, agreed to be interviewed by the right-wing newspaper *Le Matin.* In this interview of November 19th 1938 the Chief Rabbi exonerated the French government's passive attitude on the grounds of 'keeping the peace':

Unfortunately I cannot offer the slightest help in finding a solution for this most urgent problem. It is well beyond my competence. Some assistance organizations have given emigrant Jews the means to make new homes. But the Jewish problem has recently swollen to such dimensions that it can no longer be resolved within the framework of international organizations. I believe that the required solution depends far more on America and on England than on France, which has already done more than other nations and cannot cope with further immigration. I do not believe, either, that it can find a place for them in habitable parts of its colonial empire. I can only express my intention to ensure that this latest wave of persecutions will create a large movement of support for the victims.

Certainly Rabbi Weill must have been conscious of the irony implicit in summoning support from others while refusing to do anything himself, since he added: 'You must forgive me for couching the declaration which you expect in abstract terms. We cannot at this moment endorse any initiative which would endanger Franco-German understanding. No one is more sensible than I am to the suffering of 600,000 German Jews. But nothing seems to me more precious and more essential than the preservation of peace on earth.'

It is ironic to note that this scandalous interview with a representative of the Jewish community in France was fiercely denounced by Leon Blum, the man who had opposed intervention in Spain. At a banquet held by the LICA at the Aéro-Club de France on November 26th, Blum stated, amid the protracted applause of his audience: 'I can think of nothing so painful and dishonourable as to see French Jews helping to slam the doors of France in the face of Jewish refugees from other countries. They should not imagine that they will thereby preserve their own peace and security. There is no precedent in history for security achieved through cowardice [enthusiastic applause], whether by nations or other groups, or by men.'

Three weeks after the 'Crystal Night' Henri de Kerillis asked in *L'Epoque*: 'Is it credible? Herr Ribbentrop is coming to Paris to sign a declaration of Franco-German friendship. What new concessions have bought "friendship" with Hitler's Germany? The opponents of the Munich policy are anxiously wondering whether Germany has demanded and achieved the banning of the French Communist Party, and whether France has signed a "press agreement", such as those signed with Austria, Czechoslovakia, Greece and even Den-

mark, under which an internationally recognized conservative journalist was dismissed because of German diplomatic pressure.'[25]

Again, it was Bernard Lecache and the LICA that urged Parisians
to demonstrate against the scandal. Pierre Brossolette, who later paid
with his life for his opposition to Nazism, denounced the 'shameless
visit' in *Droit de Vivre* and protested at the futility of signing an
agreement with a regime that held agreements in contempt 'and is
unlikely to swoon simply because Georges Bonnet has clinked glasses
with Herr von Ribbentrop'.

In order to prevent the LICA demonstration, the Daladier government seized posters, telegrams and leaflets and intercepted material
sent out of Paris.

During this period the French Foreign Minister gave a huge banquet in honour of his counterpart from across the Rhine. Regard
for the official guest's Aryan sensitivity was carried to such extremes
that the Jewish Minister of the Colonies, Georges Mendel, and the
Protestant Minister for National Education, Jean Zay, whose ances-
tors were Jewish, were both excluded from the occasion. Edouard
Herriot declined his invitation in sympathy with them.[26]

In response to Chamberlain's request, Georges Bonnet tried to
broach the Jewish problem. The French government had not previously reacted to the stream of communications sent since August by
the Committee for Refugees which had been set up at Evian.[27]
Bonnet understood his guest's sensitivity and first raised the subject
while they were alone. Ribbentrop claimed[28] that the scene occurred
at the Hotel Crillon, where he was staying, while Bonnet claimed
that it occurred during a visit to the Louvre. Their talk, in any event,
did not overstep the bounds of an official exchange. According to the
German minister, his French colleague informed him that France
did not wish to admit further Jewish refugees into its territory and
even suggested that Berlin might take definite action to this effect,
as Switzerland had done. Bonnet confided, however, that plans were
afoot to admit the Jews into a French colony, probably Madagascar.
When Bonnet steered discussion towards the delicate matter of allowing the emigrants to take some of their property away, he was given

the same reply about the Reich's limited foreign reserves as Hitler had given the South African minister, Pirow. In conclusion, Ribbentrop stressed the private character of their talk and advised Bonnet that he would feel obliged to deny any of his statements if they were repeated by the French press.

This statement, symptomatic of the arrogance with which the Nazis habitually conducted their diplomacy, combined with the barrage of insults which the German minister flung at the Jews, did not deter Georges Bonnet from reporting in an account of his meeting which he gave to the American chargé d'affaires in Paris that 'Ribbentrop personally regretted the way in which the German authorities had treated the Jewish problem recently and that Ribbentrop would be disposed to assist in so far as he could in efforts to handle this problem on a more reasonable basis.'[29]

It is clear, however, that German diplomacy successfully neutralized France and short-circuited hopes for an indispensable united effort by the Western Powers. Concerted action would have been all the more feasible in the light of British public opinion, whose demands were echoed by the Americans.

On November 14th Under Secretary of State George Messersmith had sent an urgent request to Secretary of State Cordell Hull, whose wife was, in fact, Jewish, as the German Ambassador to the United States did not fail to underscore in his report to his government. Describing the Nazi government's assaults on defenceless people, Messersmith wrote: 'We have throughout our history let it be known where we stand on matters of principle and the decencies. We have not failed to do this recently. Whenever such acts in the past have been committed, or permitted by Governments, in countries which the world has considered less civilized, we have spoken and acted. . . . It is my belief that unless we take some action in the face of the events in Germany of the last few days we shall be much behind our public opinion in this country. We shall run a grave risk of losing the leadership of opinion which our Government now has and this at a time when this leadership is all important in our most vital interests.'[30]

Messersmith suggested that the American Ambassador to Berlin be recalled immediately 'for consultation', and that President Roosevelt give a press conference on the recall without commenting on it. He was certain that the press would unanimously approve this gesture and that it would have a strong impact on public opinion. 'It is my further considered opinion that the country is waiting for something of this kind and that not doing it will be a definite letdown and set us back in our general stand and policy.'

His proposal was accepted. The same day Cordell Hull cabled Ambassador Wilson in Berlin: 'You should plan to sail on the first available non-German ship.'[81] Two days later the American Ambassador left the German capital and embarked at Cherbourg. Although he had merely been 'recalled for consultation', this unusual and spectacular decision by the White House left a deep impression on the rest of the world and nettled the German leaders. Hitler, exasperated by 'President Roosevelt's incessant insults', considered economic retaliation, but his advisers informed him that such measures would harm Germany more than the United States, since German imports from that country consisted mainly of raw materials (petroleum and its derivatives, copper and cotton) and a break with the United States would cause a serious setback in the German rearmament programme. These considerations heightened Hitler's anxiety. The Nazi leaders feared that the Americans might follow their example and expel German nationals resident in the United States. Goering suggested that they might eventually exchange the German Jews for persons of German origin from the United States.

But the German leaders were needlessly alarmed. Messersmith had already charted the limits of the American reaction in his memorandum of November 14th: 'Calling back our Ambassador "for consultation" cannot interfere in any way with our relations, political or commercial, with Germany and our interests in Germany will not suffer.' The American gesture was aimed at German public opinion, and still more, as Messersmith himself guilelessly expressed it, at maintaining leadership over American public opinion, which had been outraged by the 'Crystal Night'.

'The outcry comes not only from Jews,' noted the German Ambassador to Washington in a report to Ribbentrop, 'but in equal strength from all camps and classes, including the German-American camp.'[32]

In fact, the State Department in Washington was swamped with articles from the press, protest messages from Protestant and Catholic organizations and trade unions, resolutions adopted at meetings in Cincinnati, Minneapolis, Kansas City, Washington, Boston, Memphis, New York, Spokane and Detroit, letters from the Non-Sectarian Anti-Nazi League, and messages from various American universities. Private individuals even sent telegrams to Cordell Hull. A telegram from a Mrs Catt asked, 'How long will the Christian world permit the barbarous and uncivilized treatment of innocent people in Germany to continue? Nothing I have ever read in the history of civilization can equal the horror of what is happening in Europe today. The United States must voice its protest in the name of civilization itself.'[33]

Contrary opinions were few. Father Proeller, Rector of the Pallotine House of Studies in Washington, reproached the government for not having protested with equal vigour at the persecution of the Catholic minority in Mexico or when 'between 12,000 and 15,000 priests, sisters and seminarians, all non-combatants, were brutally murdered and ravished by the Communistic followers of the so-called Spanish government'.[34] A certain Ferdinand Hansen, who claimed to be president of Romano Caviars, distributed a leaflet in California stating that the plight of the German Jews could not be compared with the treatment which the victors at Versailles had meted out to the defeated and starving German population at the end of the First World War.[35]

On November 15th 1938 more than two hundred journalists assembled at the White House to hear the President's announcement. Roosevelt followed Messersmith's suggestion and confined himself to a short statement prepared in advance. He expressed the shock which events in Germany had caused, and announced that the American Ambassador to Berlin was being recalled for consultation.

The journalists were disappointed by the President's reticence and plied him with questions. What would happen to the refugees? The International Committee (of Evian) would look after them. Had the President any idea which country these refugees would go to? He had considered the matter at length but was not yet prepared to make a statement. A journalist asked if the President would recommend that Congress amend the immigration laws so that the United States could admit more refugees. The answer was negative. The United States stubbornly indulged in bad faith in this matter until it was too late to undertake any large-scale rescue operation.

The Jewish organizations proposed that the immigration quotas of future years should be set against the current year. They suggested that 82,000 refugees be admitted immediately and, to offset this, that German immigration be suspended for the next three years. But the proposal was rejected.

Great Britain informed President Roosevelt, through Sumner Welles, that it was prepared to forgo 65,000 places in its American immigration quota on behalf of Jewish refugees. Welles described the legal and political obstacles. 'I added that it was my very strong impression,' he said in his report to the Department of State, 'that the responsible leaders among American Jews would be the first to urge that no change in the present quota for German Jews be made.'[86]

These legal obstacles were, however, no more than a pretext. A few days after his categorical statements, President Roosevelt made the gesture of disregarding all the rules by authorizing some twelve to fifteen thousand Jews (including a number of scientists, artists and university teachers) who had entered the United States with tourist visas to renew their visas at six-monthly intervals for as long as was necessary until they could adopt American citizenship.

President Roosevelt was aware that, despite the protests, American public opinion would balk at an influx of refugees. A poll conducted a few months after the 'Crystal Night' asked: 'If you were a member of Congress would you vote "yes" or "no" on a bill to open the doors

f the United States to a larger number of European refugees than
now admitted under our immigration quotas?' Eighty-three per cent
were against such a bill and 8.3 per cent did not know. Of the 8.7
per cent in favour, nearly 70 per cent were Jewish.[87]

At the very time when sympathy for the victims was at its height,
ten Americans out of eleven opposed massive Jewish immigration
into the United States. Some intellectuals, including such writers as
Eugene O'Neill, John Steinbeck, Pearl Buck, Clifford Odets and
Thornton Wilder, tried to illustrate the immorality of the American
attitude: 'Thirty-five years ago, a horrified America rose in protest
against the pogrom at Kishinev in Tsarist Russia. God have pity on
us if we have become so insensitive to human suffering that we are
incapable of protesting today against the pogroms in Nazi Germany.
We believe it is profoundly immoral for the Americans to continue
to maintain commercial relations with a country which openly
adopts mass murder to solve its economic problems.'[88]

Isolated voices within the American administration expressed the
same anguish. One of the most forceful was that of Anthony Drexel
Biddle, Jr, the American Ambassador to Warsaw, who sent dispatch
after dispatch to his superiors informing them that according to
reliable sources the Nazis were aware that their action had aroused
world-wide indignation but understood that no one would lift a
finger to oppose them. This assessment was correct, since the European Affairs Section of the State Department, which was asked to
elaborate the American Government's position on the matter, merely
formulated an official confession of impotence. 'It is easy to put the
problem aside by declaring that no one wants more Jews. This is
certainly true, but the problem must nevertheless be solved and our
government has committed itself. . . .

'Regardless of what we may feel individually about the Jews,
the suffering which these people have had to endure cannot fail
to touch the humanitarian instincts of the most hardened individual.'[89]

Despite the burning synagogues, the terror of the 'Crystal Night'
and the desperate appeals for help from Jewish groups, the countries

which could help followed the lead of the three great western power
They continued the pointless charade, begun at the Evian Confe
ence, of searching for the elusive country which would agree to tal
in refugees. On November 23rd President Roosevelt sent Myro
Taylor a confidential letter instructing him immediately to rene
the efforts of the Intergovernmental Committee for Refugees, calle
the Evian Committee. 'It is essential,' Roosevelt wrote, 'to crea
the proper spirit in the countries of potential settlement and to lea
them to see this problem as one which is humanitarian in its urgen
but from which they can draw ultimate practical benefit. . . . I o
not believe it either desirable or practicable to recommend any chan;
in the quota provisions of our immigration laws. We are prepare
nevertheless, to make any other contribution which may be in o
power to make.'[40]

This message assumes greater significance when one conside
that on the same day, November 23rd 1938, the American new
papers re-published an extract from *Das Schwarze Korps* whi
unequivocally announced Hitler's intention of finding a 'totalitari
solution' for the Jewish problem, including the eradication of Je
from the economy and their isolation in ghettoes so as to redu
them to misery and crime. The official SS and Gestapo publicatio
which had been the first to prime public opinion for the pogroms
November 1938, concluded genially: 'At this stage of developme
we should therefore face the hard necessity of exterminating t
Jewish underworld in the same fashion in which in this state of ord
we exterminate criminals generally – by fire and sword.'[41]

This was the last announcement before the Nazis sprang in
action. It provoked no reaction. The American journalist Arth
Morse has described in detail the fruitless negotiations undertak
by representatives of Western nations with the Nazi leaders at t
very moment when the cattle trains began to haul away th
Jewish cargo to fiercer conflagrations than those of the 'Crys
Night'.[42]

The curtain fell on the tragedy. The audience had not understo
that it was the prelude to an infinitely greater, more lethal traged

which many of them would in turn become the abandoned ctims.

Like the chorus in a Greek tragedy, the voice of another oppressed :ople, in India, drew a lesson from this drama: 'There is something tten in Western civilization. The poison has not infected Germany one. It has infected many other governments. It infects people, td not only the German people. This poison must be rooted out!' .mritza Bazar Patrika, Calcutta, November 13th 1938).

Epilogue: the Fate of Grynszpan

Though Grynszpan's ultimate fate remains unknown, his story ca
be traced for over two years after the terrible events of Novembe
1938, which he involuntarily set in train.

When the outbreak of the Second World War seemed to offe
De Moro-Giafferi some hope of winning an acquittal for Grynszpa
a lawyer from Geneva, Marcel Guinand, intervened on behalf of th
Germans to request an adjournment of the trial *sine die*, which w:
granted by the Attorney General. There now began for Grynszpa
a long, anxious period of suspense. From his prison cell he showere
De Moro-Giafferi with letters (some friendly, some pleading, a fe
threatening), most of which were never answered. Grynszpan fe
that his lawyer had grown indifferent and appealed for help to Henr
Torrès, who was unable to do more than pay a few visits.[1] De Mor
Giafferi only visited him once, on February 17th 1940, to tell hi
that his request for immediate trial or release had been refused. Th
same request was refused again in March by the Public Prosecuto
who did not respond at all the following month when Victor Basch
President of the League of Human Rights, submitted a demand fc
'freedom or trial' for Grynszpan. The consequence was a uniqu
event in French legal history: Grynszpan was held in preventiv
custody for twenty months. The Public Prosecutor told De Mor

Giafferi that further progress, either by beginning the trial or by granting provisional release, would arouse formidable opposition 'of which it was not his responsibility to uncover the source'.

The pace of military events after May 15th 1940 tended to spur the matter forward against the manifest resistance of the French authorities. By June 1st the government was impelled to plan the withdrawal of judicial personnel and the evacuation of prisons. The Court of Paris was to withdraw to Angers. Prisoners from Paris were to be moved south. Grynszpan found himself in a convoy from Fresnes prison bound for Orléans. As the Germans advanced, he and ninety-six other prisoners were evacuated to Bourges. In the convoy between Orléans and Bourges the escort bolted during a German air-raid and the prisoners were left to their own devices. Most of them dispersed into the open country without further ado, but a few of them, including Grynszpan, who feared capture by the Germans, asked to be taken to Bourges prison. They arrived on June 17th, guarded by an unidentified sub-officer whose subsequent indiscretion was the opening of a fresh drama.

Bourges prison gradually ceased to be a prison as confusion mounted on the French roads and in towns before the rapid advance of the German army. It became a reception centre where families were reunited after being separated in flight. The Germans pressed steadily forward. On the morning of June 18th the prison warden approached the Public Prosecutor of Bourges, Paul Ribeyre, to ask what should be done with prisoners from Orléans, including Grynszpan. On the advice of the Chief of Police, Taviani, Ribeyre cautioned the warden to be certain not to enter Grynszpan's name in the prison register and to let him 'slip away' by the only route still open: the Châteauroux road.[8] Grynszpan accepted all his instructions and reported to Châteauroux prison, where he was again sent southwards. Finally he arrived alone and free at Toulouse.

The Germans had not forgotten 'the Jew Grynszpan.' In the early hours of June 19th some officers who had been following him arrived at Bourges prison with the request that the 'criminal' be handed over. The warden claimed not to recognize the name and never to have

had any such prisoner. The Germans thus lost scent of their pre
But their bloodhounds were soon in pursuit again. They traced an
found the sub-officer who had escorted Grynszpan from Orléans t
Bourges. Under their grilling he quickly lost his nerve and stammere
out what he was supposed to have concealed: that he had broug
Grynszpan to Bourges prison. The German military police blame
Public Prosecutor Ribeyre for Grynszpan's escape and kept hi
under surveillance while awaiting further instructions from Pari
His villa in Rue Calvin was placed under guard and, grotesque
enough, the guard beguiled the hours playing records, one of whic
was 'All is very Well, Madame la Marquise'. A German car blocke
the door of the Public Prosecutor's garage, preventing him fro
using his car. The Chief of Police, however, managed to outwit th
German guard and met Ribeyre. He told him what he had said t
the Germans when he himself was interrogated by them, and advise
Ribeyre to corroborate both his story and the prison warden's, re
vealing no more than that the prisoners for whom there had been n
room at Bourges had been taken to Châteauroux.

On June 30th, after the German military police at Bourges ha
fumbled over transfers and interrogations, Ribeyre was conducte
to Paris under heavy guard. The party halted *en route* to mak
inquiries at the prison in Orléans. In Paris, Ribeyre was locked in
windowless cell in Cherche-Midi Prison. His whereabouts were ke
secret until July 11th, when a German officer questioned hi
through an interpreter and then informed him that he would b
executed in three hours. When he returned to his cell Ribeyre fe
a sudden calm replace the hustle and anxiety of the preceding day
He wrote a farewell letter to his family and another letter assumin
full responsibility for Grynszpan's transfer to Châteauroux and ex
culpating the warden of Bourges prison. Three hours later nothin
happened. That night and the following day, July 12th, Ribey
waited for death. At about eleven o'clock on the morning of th
13th two armed soldiers took him back to the room where he ha
been questioned. Here, to his amazement, he found the Publi
Prosecutor of Paris, who informed him that he could expect to b

eleased soon. It was only then that he learned that Grynszpan, who had been tracked down at Toulouse prison, would have to be handed over to the Germans according to Article 19 of the Franco-German Armistice convention. Ribeyre was freed on July 15th. In recognition of his courageous conduct, and as a safeguard against any further entanglement with the Germans, the Chancellor of the Vichy government, Alibert, assigned him to the Public Prosecutor's office in Algiers. Ribeyre's unnerving ordeal finished as Grynszpan's was just beginning.

Grynszpan's file had been delivered a month before on June 15th to the office of Dr Helmut Knochen at the Hotel du Louvre in Paris, and added to the heap of records relating to German emigrés who had opposed the Nazi regime, most of whom were Jews. Knochen, who with Oberg was to be recorded in history as 'the butcher of Paris', was known as a 'cultivated sportsman'; he was a doctor of philosophy and could claim credit for the implementation of Heydrich's audacious scheme to abduct two British officers in peacetime from Dutch territory – the notorious Venlo incident. Under his command, SS Sturmbannführer Karl Bömelburg was put in charge of the Grynszpan case. Bömelburg had been the Interpol link between the German Embassy and French Police Headquarters and was already conversant with the details of the case.

The German police now sprang into action. The Sturmbann-führer's first and most difficult task was to locate Grynszpan and his record. After inquiries failed in Paris and at prosecutors' offices in Orléans and Bourges, he approached the Commanding Officers at police headquarters and suggested that they forward a request to Vichy (where the German Occupation Force as yet had no representative), asking the Vichy government simply to hand Grynszpan over to the German police. The suggestion reached Vichy just as the news broke of Ribeyre's arrest and of the unexpected discovery of Grynszpan in Toulouse prison.

Grynszpan had arrived in Toulouse without escort. He was penniless, however, and spoke French with a thick German accent. As he could not survive in an unfamiliar country without some help, he endured his freedom for only a fortnight. Then he was unable to resolve his difficulties except by giving himself up at Toulouse prison where he was taken in (as he had not been at Bourges). In fact Grynszpan showed a lack not just of initiative, but of common sense He should have been able to reckon with the political changes which had occurred in France after the Armistice and he should have seized his unbelievable opportunity to go to ground in the surrounding country or to seek help. By an extraordinary coincidence, help was literally within reach. As the German armies closed in on the capital, most of the Parisian Jews naturally grew apprehensive and fled southwards. Grynszpan's Uncle Abraham and his wife, his Uncle Berenbaum and one of his lawyers, Isidore Fränkel, had all come to Toulouse, while De Moro-Giafferi had headed for Aiguillon in the province of Lot-et-Garonne not far away. In Toulouse Grynszpan had literally returned to the fold of his family and his lawyers. Un fortunately, he did not know any of this. Just as he was about to be taken from Toulouse prison, Fränkel happened to find out where he was and tried to arrange to see him. By the following day, however when authorization for the visit arrived from the Public Prosecutor Grynszpan had been removed.

At the Germans' request, the Vichy government had searched the prisons in the Free Zone. Soon afterwards Otto Abetz, the German Minister Plenipotentiary in Paris, was able to telegraph to Berlin the news that the Vichy Minister of Justice had located Grynszpan in Toulouse prison. The German lawyer Friedrich Grimm, who had been assigned to follow Grynszpan's case from the beginning, rushed to Paris to demand Grynszpan's extradition from Vichy. He invoked Article 19 of the Franco-German Armistice Convention, under which the Vichy government was obliged to hand over to the Nazi authori ties all German subjects (whether Jews, socialists, communists or other opponents of the Nazi regime) who had taken refuge in France.

The Vichy government did not attempt to play for time either by raising legal objections against Grynszpan's extradition or by ques tioning the German lawyer Grimm's authority to make the request Grynszpan was delivered straight into the Nazis' hands. Otto

Abetz sent a triumphant telegram to Berlin: 'Upon German request Grynszpan was brought to the German representatives at the line of demarcation today, July 18th 1940, to be transferred to Berlin.'[4]

Two months later the *New York Times* criticized the Vichy Government's action. Under a banner headline, 'Grynszpan, Who Killed Nazi, Is Given Up To German Secret Police by Vichy Official', the newspaper reported that Herschel Grynszpan, the young Polish Jew who assassinated a Nazi diplomat and touched off Germany's unprecedented November, 1938, persecutions of Jews, has been delivered into the hands of the Gestapo [secret police] by the government of Marshal Henri Philippe Pétain and Pierre Laval.'[5]

This cowardly act, which made a mockery of any legal regulations relating to political exiles, launched the Pétain–Laval government on a course of dishonourable collaboration which was to seal the fate not only of political refugees of German origin, but of the Jewish men, women and children of France, the patriots and the Resistance fighters who refused to tolerate Nazism.

In Berlin young Grynszpan underwent a relatively mild interrogation by the Gestapo before being sent on January 18th 1941 to the concentration camp at Sachsenhausen. Here he was given preferential treatment, compared with the majority of the inmates, because his co-operation would be needed in the sensational trial which Dr Goebbels' staff were planning for him. In the summer of 1941, as the Prosecutor of the People's Tribunal, Ernst Lautz, was drawing up the formal charge against Grynszpan which was to be the centrepiece of the trial, Grynszpan was transferred from Sachsenhausen to the Gestapo prison in Berlin-Moabit.

German law disqualified the German courts from trying a political crime committed outside Germany by a stateless person. The Reich Minister of Justice side-stepped this difficulty by accusing Grynszpan of 'intention to commit high treason with the purpose of preventing by force, or by threat of force, the Führer and Chancellor of the Reich and the members of his government from exercising the powers accorded them under the constitution'. A charge of 'high treason' placed the case within the jurisdiction of the German courts and carried the death penalty.

At a ministers' meeting, representatives of the Ministry of Justice and the Ministry of Propaganda fixed the date of Grynszpan's trial for February 18th 1942. They intended to bring the former French Foreign Minister, Georges Bonnet, to the witness stand to attest to the collusion of world Jewry. It was reckoned in Berlin that Bonnet would offer his co-operation, despite the outcome of the war between France and Germany.

'I shall take care,' Goebbels wrote in his journal, 'to ensure that Bonnet's testimony, an essential part of which puts the blame on the Jews for the outbreak of war, will be properly prepared [sic] so that we may gain a great victory for our side.'[6]

The ever-available Friedrich Grimm paid a visit to the Paris home of Edouard Daladier's former minister and tried to persuade him to testify at Grynszpan's trial. On December 22nd 1941 he reported, obviously prematurely, on the success of his mission to Ribbentrop, the German Foreign Minister. 'M. Georges Bonnet,' he advised Counsellor Albrecht, 'has expressed full agreement with me on all the points I raised and is willing, in principle, to testify at the trial.'[7]

Grimm, whose imagination was as fevered as his exertions, conceived the further plan of 'inviting' the French examining magistrate Tesnière to the witness box as well. By the most unlikely coincidence Grimm had learned that the French judge, who had been in charge of Grynszpan's case in Paris until 1939, was an officer in a German prisoner-of-war camp. Grimm made contact with him and reported to the Gestapo in Berlin that Tesnière seemed willing to collaborate with the Nazi judiciary authorities in exchange for his freedom.[8] According to the testimony of Dr A. Cuenot,[9] however, Judge Tesnière, who was relased for medical reasons in December 1940, wrote to him after 1945 categorically denying that he had struck such a bargain with Friedrich Grimm.

Despite the feverish preparations at the Ministries of Justice and Propaganda, the Grynszpan trial had to be postponed because the date chosen for its opening, February 18th 1942, happened to over-lap with the equally sensational Riom trials. These had been under-taken by the Vichy government in order to try prominent men of the Third Republic held responsible for the defeat of France, including Léon Blum, Edouard Daladier, Paul Reynaud and General Gamelin. The master mind of German propaganda calculated that it would be pointless for the trial of 'World Jewry' to compete against the trial of the men of the French Third Republic. The Nazis decided to postpone the Grynszpan trial. Grimm approached Marshal Pétain to find out when he expected the Riom trials to finish, so that the Germans would know when to begin theirs.[10] After consultation Hitler agreed to a new date for Grynszpan's trial: May 11th 1942.

As it happened, Grynszpan found a means to balk the German machine and the trial never took place. He claimed to have had homosexual relations with Counsellor vom Rath and that these had played an important part in motivating his crime.

'Grynszpan,' Goebbels wrote in his journal, 'has insolently in-vented a homosexual liaison with Embassy Counsellor vom Rath. It is nothing other than a shameless fabrication. But it is a lucky inspira-tion for him, since if it were brought out in a trial it would become a dominant theme in adverse propaganda.'[11]

Ribbentrop favoured launching the trial notwithstanding, but Goebbels was concerned lest a scandal be provoked by this 'absurd and typically Jewish claim' of sexual relations between a shabby little Polish Jew and a handsome Aryan diplomat of the Third Reich. He obtained an indefinite postponement of the trial.

In January 1966 Franz Schlegelberger, former Vice-Minister of Justice, testified at the trial of Wolfgang Diewerge, who had been one of Goebbels' principal aides in dealing with the Grynszpan case, that the leaders of the Third Reich wanted to turn the Grynszpan trial into a justification for the 'final solution'.[12] There is no documentary evidence to sustain this claim, but a theory expounded in the com-munist newspaper *L'Humanité* in 1938[13] is supported by documents and by the facts themselves: that just as the fire started by Marinus van der Lubbe in February 1933 offered the Nazis the ideal pretext for persecuting the communists, so Herschel Grynszpan's act of vengeance of November 1938 gave them the ideal pretext for a witch-hunt against the German Jews.

The ultimate fate of Grynszpan himself has never been determined. Some, including his family, claim that he was executed by the Nazis, while others believed that he survived and assumed a false identity at the end of the war.

Notes to the Text

ABBREVIATIONS

DBRFP   Documents on British Foreign Policy 1919–39, Series 2 and 3
(HMSO, London)

DGFP   Documents on German Foreign Policy 1918–1945: Series C
1933–1937, and D, 1937–1945 (H.M.S.O., London, and
Washington)

DZA   Deutsches Zentralarchiv (Central Archives of the German
Democratic Republic, Potsdam)

FRUS   Foreign Relations of the United States (Documents edited by
the Department of State, Washington)

IMT   Trial of the Major War Criminals before the International
Military Tribunal. Nuremberg 14 November 1945–1 October
1946 [proceedings and documents] (42 vols, Nuremberg,
1947–49)

CHAPTER 1

1 IMT, Vol. XXXII, Doc. 3358–PS.
2 Hossbach testimony, November 10th 1937, IMT, Vol. XXV, Doc.
386–PS, pp. 402–413.
3 For statistics on Jewish emigration from Germany, see Werner
Rosenstock, 'Exodus 1933–39', in *Leo Baeck Institute Yearbook*, I (London,
1956), pp. 373–90, which lists the major sources and published studies.
4 *Reichsgesetzblatt*, 1938, I, pp. 414 ff.
5 See FRUS 1938, II, pp. 366–80.
6 Wiener Library, London, Doc. P II d no. 325 and P II d no. 760.

CRYSTAL NIGHT

7 Bernard Kolb (secretary of the Jewish congregation in Nuremberg until he emigrated), *History of the Jews of Nuremberg*, Wiener Library, Doc. P II e no. 765.

8 Minutes of the Municipal Council of Nuremberg, August 3rd 1938 (City Archives).

9 Actes du Comité Intergouvernemental pour les réfugiés, Evian, du 6 au 15 juillet 1938 (Paris, 1938), p. 13.

10 *Ibid.*, p. 20.

11 Weltgeschichte der Gegenwart in Dokumenten (Herder Verlag), I, p. 71.

12 See Joseph L. Tenenbaum, *The Crucial Year 1938*, pp. 53–56; Alfred A. Häsler, *Das Boot ist voll* (2nd ed., Zurich and Stuttgart, 1968); Eliahu Ben Elissar, *La Diplomatie du IIIe Reich et les Juifs 1933–1939* (Paris, 1969), pp. 267–80.

13 *Reichsgesetzblatt*, I, p. 1342.

14 Memorandum of October 14th 1938, Inland II A/B Juden ausw. A. A. Bonn, cited by Eliahu Ben Elissar, *op. cit.*, p. 262.

15 Jochen Klepper, *Unter dem Schatten deiner Flügel* (DVA, Stuttgart, 1955, ed. of 1962), p. 631.

16 Hans Globke, born in 1898, was a high-ranking official in the Ministry of the Interior who drafted the commentary on the Nuremberg Racial Laws (1935) and 'negotiated' the expulsion of the Jews from the Sudeten territories in November 1938. After the war he became Secretary of State and Chancellor Adenauer's 'grey eminence'.

17 IMT, Vol. XXVII, Doc. 1301–PS.

18 Ibid., Vol. XXXII, Doc. 3545–PS.

19 Wiener Library, London, Doc. P II d no. 760, and Lionel Kochan, *Pogrom, 10 November 1938* (London, 1957).

20 Related by Goering during the meeting of November 12th 1938. IMT, Vol. XXVIII, Doc. 1816–PS.

21 Telegram from Halifax to Newton, October 20th 1938, and reply Newton to Halifax, October 22nd 1938. DBRFP, Third Series, Vol. III, pp. 195–6.

22 See Richard Coudenhove-Kalergi, *Judenhass* (Paneuropa Verlag, 1937), and Eliahu Ben Elissar, *op. cit.*, pp. 301–321.

23 Message from Gaus to the German Ambassador to Poland, DGFP, Series D, V, pp. 111–12.

24 DGFP, Series D, V, no. 91, p. 118.

25 Reichministerium für Volksaufklärung und Propaganda, File 982 F 4–6, DZA, Potsdam.

26 Wiener Library, London, Doc. P III c no. 646.
27 *Ibid.*, Doc. P III c no. 630.

CHAPTER 2

1 Reichsministerium für Volksaufklärung und Propaganda, File 991 F 54–55, DZA, Potsdam.
2 The year 1911 was the period of the Beilis case. Accused of the ritual murder of a Christian child, Beilis was arrested and tried at Kiev, but then, to general astonishment, was acquitted.
3 *Eichmann Trial*, fourteenth sitting, April 25th 1961, Yad Washem Institute, Jerusalem.
4 David Frankfurter was tried at Coire in the Canton of Grisons, where there was neither capital punishment nor life imprisonment. He was sentenced to eighteen years' hard labour. Released in 1945, he now lives in Israel. See also Jean Pierre-Bloch and Didier Meran, *L'Affair Frankfurter* (Paris, 1937).
5 Memorandum on the Grynszpan case by vom Rath's father, archives of Dr A. Cuenot, Arcachon.
6 Wolfgang Diewerge, *Anschlag gegen den Frieden* (Munich, 1939), p. 50.
7 Havas Report, no. 13 Special, November 7th 1938.
8 Havas Report no. 32 Special, November 7th 1938.
9 *L'Oeuvre*, November 8th 1938.
10 *Le Temps*, November 15th 1938 and November 17th 1938.
11 *Ibid.*, November 18th 1938.
12 Reichsministerium für Volksaufklärung und Propaganda, File no. 979 F 49, DZA, Potsdam.
13 *New York Herald Tribune*, November 16th 1938.
14 *Der Angriff*, November 19th 1938.
15 Dr Genil-Perrin, Dr Ceillier and Dr Heuer.
16 Medico–legal Report, February 2nd 1939, Reichsministerium für Volksaufklärung und Propaganda, File no. 989 F 23–38, DZA, Potsdam; archives of Dr A. Cuenot, Arcachon.
17 Memorandum on the Grynszpan case by vom Rath's father, archives of Dr A. Cuenot, Arcachon.
18 'Les Instructions Secrètes de la Propagande Allemande', pamphlet published by *Le Petit Parisien* (1937). See files at the Centre de Documentation Juive Contemporaine, Paris.
19 Bills and Reports on the Action, Reichsministerium für Volksaufklärung und Propaganda, File no. 979 F 81, DZA, Potsdam.

20 Reichministerium für Volksaufklärung und Propaganda, File no. 983 F 68, DZA, Potsdam.

CHAPTER 3

1 See *Der Angriff*, November 9th 1938.
2 Wiener Library, London, Doc. P II d no. 729.
3 IMT, Vol. XII, p. 381.
4 *Ibid.*, Vol. XXXII, Doc. 3063–PS, pp. 20–29.
5 *Ibid.*, Vol. XIV, p. 422, Vol. XX, p. 293, Vol. XII, p. 326.
6 Friedrich Christian, Prinz zu Schaumburg-Lippe, *Zwischen Krone und Kerker* (Wiesbaden, 1952), pp. 256–8.
7 Otto Dietrich, *Zwölf Jahre mit Hitler* (Munich, 1955), pp. 55–56.
8 IMT, Vol. XXV, Doc. 374–PS, pp. 376–80.
9 Orders of the SA Commander of the 'Baltic Group' in Scheffler-Schwarze, 'Broadcast for Brotherhood Week in R.F.A.', Wiener Library, London.
10 IMT, Vol. XXXI, Doc. 3051–PS, pp. 515–19.
11 Wiener Library, London, Doc. B 83.
12 *Ibid.*, Docs B 341 and B 42.
13 Report of the American Consul David H. Buffum of November 21st 1938, Doc. L 202, in *Nazi Conspiracy and Aggression* (8 vols, Office of United States Chief of Counsel for Prosecution of Axis Criminality, United States Government Printing Office, Washington, 1946), Vol. VII, pp. 1037–41.
14 IMT, Doc. 2604–PS, in *ibid.*, Vol. V, p. 312.
15 Wiener Library, London, Docs B 23 and B 67.
16 *Ibid.*, Docs P II e no. 765 and B 65.
17 *Dokumente über die Verfolgung der Jüd. Bürger in Baden-Württemberg 1933–1945* (Stuttgart, 1966) Vol. 2, pp. 31–33.
18 *Ibid.*, pp. 29–30.
19 Heinrich von Treitschke (1834–96), who wrote a history of Germany in the nineteenth century in five volumes, was one of the historians of Prussian imperialism who inspired generations of nationalists.
20 Adolf Stoecker (1835–1909), Protestant preacher at the court of Wilhelm II, was the founder, among others, of the Christian Social Party which disseminated antisemitic doctrines among the middle classes.
21 Kurt Meier, *Kirche und Judentum* (Halle, 1968), p. 33.
22 Wilhelm Niemoeller, *Kampf und Zeugnis der Bekennenden Kirche* (Bielefeld, 1948), p. 458.

23 Wiener Library, London, Doc. P II d no. 93.
24 *Dokumente z. Geschichte der Frankfurter Juden 1933–45* (Frankfurt am Main, 1963); Yad Washem Institute, Jerusalem, Doc. 1081/111; Wiener Library, London, Docs P II d no. 1215 and B 131.
25 Wiener Library, London, Doc. P II d no. 151.

CHAPTER 4

1 IMT, Vol. XXXI, Doc. 3051–PS, pp. 518–19.
2 *Ibid.*, Vol. XXVII, Doc. 1721–PS, pp. 487–8.
3 *Völkischer Beobachter*, November 12th 1938.
4 IMT, Vol. XXVIII, Doc. 1757–PS, pp. 55–234.
5 Partial reproduction of the transcript of the meeting, IMT, Vol. XXVIII, Doc. 1816–PS, pp. 499–540.
6 On the spoliation of the Jews in Germany see Helmut Genschel's excellent study *Die Verdrängung der Juden aus der Wirtschaft im III. Reich* (Göttingen, 1966).
7 IMT, Vol. XXVII, Doc. 1721–PS, p. 486.
8 This was Article 7 of the decree on Jewish wealth of April 26th 1938.
9 In Germany the mandatory declaration of assets (above 5,000 marks) amounted to 7,500 million marks, of which 7,000 million belonged to 136,000 German Jews and the balance to 9,500 foreign Jews. (Wiehl Documents, Diplomatic Archives, Bonn, cited by Eliahu Ben Elissar, *La Diplomatie du IIIe Reich et les Juifs 1933–1939*, Paris, 1969, p. 240).
10 This is, again, the decree on Jewish wealth of April 26th 1938.
11 The idea of a Jewish reservation on Madagascar had already been broached by Paul de Lagarde, a notorious antisemite of the Bismarck era. It was mentioned again in a German pamphlet of 1927. Then, in 1937, the Polish government sounded out the French Minister of the Colonies, Marius Moutet; they even sent a group of experts to the island and informed the American State Department that they had done so. As Goering indicated, it was on November 9th 1938 that Hitler in his turn took up the Polish proposal. See Eliahu Ben Elissar, *op. cit.*, pp. 407–411.

CHAPTER 5

1 The statistics for Dachau and Buchenwald have been supplied by the Centre for Documentation at Arolsen. The figures for Sachsenhausen have been estimated.

2 Wiener Library, London, Docs B 69 and B 145.
3 *Ibid.*, Docs B 8, B 77, B 194, B 323.
4 *Ibid.*, Scheffler-Schwarz radio broadcast.
5 *Ibid.*, Doc. B 77.
6 *Ibid.*, Doc. B 346.
7 *Ibid.*, Doc. B 323.
8 *Ibid.*, Doc. B 152.
9 Speech by Emil Carlebach at the commemoration of the thirtieth anniversary of the 'Crystal Night' organized by the Échanges Franco-Allemands in Paris on December 13th 1968. See the report in *Rencontres franco-allemandes*, Paris, January–February 1969, pp. 4–8.
10 Wiener Library, London, Doc. P II d no. 420.
11 *Ibid.*, Doc. P III h no. 1105.
12 *Ibid.*, *loc. cit.*
13 Testimony of Hans Block, formerly a lawyer in Hanover, Yad Washem Institute, Jerusalem, Doc. 583/55.
14 Testimony of Peter Zadek, interned in Buchenwald from November 10th 1938 to February 10th 1939. Wiener Library, London, Doc. P II d no. 45.

CHAPTER 6

1 Report of the American Ambassador to Poland, Drexel Biddle Jr, November 15th 1938, Department of State Doc. no. 862.4016/1961.
2 Report of the American Ambassador to Greece, November 16th 1938, Department of State Doc. no. 862. 4016/2027.
3 *Diario de Noticias*, Lisbon, November 16th 1938.
4 *Politiken*, Copenhagen, November 13th 1938.
5 Report of the American Ambassador to Sweden, November 18th 1938, Department of State Doc. no. 862. 4016/1990.
6 *Le Monde*, January 24th–25th 1971. See also Alfred A. Häsler, *Das Boot ist voll* (Zurich, 1967).
7 Report by Kirk, American chargé d'affaires to Moscow, November 25th 1938, Department of State Doc. no. 862.4016/1902.
8 Kurt R. Grossmann, *Emigration* (Frankfurt am Main, 1969), p. 107.
9 *Der Angriff*, Berlin, November 8th 1938.
10 Telegram from Strang to Ogilvie-Forbes, no. 521, November 9th 1938. Replies: telegram from Ogilvie-Forbes, no. 662, November 10th 1938; telegram no. 681, November 13th 1938; telegram no. 693, November 15th 1938. In DBRFP, Third Series, Vol. III, pp. 264–72.

11 Michael Bruce, *Tramp Royal* (London, 1954), pp. 236–40.
12 Letter from H. von Dirksen, no. A 4706, November 17th 1938, DGFP, Series D, IV, pp. 332–4.
13 *Liverpool Weekly Post*, November 19th 1938.
14 Parliamentary Debates, House of Commons, Official Report, Vol. 341, no. 10, November 21st 1938.
15 *Völkischer Beobachter*, November 12th 1938.
16 On the Pirow mission, see Joseph L. Tenenbaum, *The Crucial Year*, and Eliahu Ben Elissar, *La Diplomatie du IIIe Reich et les Juifs 1933–1939* (Paris, 1969), pp. 365–8.
17 Note by Hewel, November 24th 1938, DGFP, Series D, IV, p. 339.
18 Telegram from Mackensen, no. 313, November 28th 1938, DGFP, Series D, IV, p. 342.
19 Minutes of Franco-British talks of November 24th 1938, in DBRFP, Third Series, Vol. III, pp. 294–6.
20 *Action Française*, November 8th 1938.
21 Telegram from Gray, Paris, November 14th 1938, Department of State Doc. no. 862.4016/1819.
22 Emile Buré, 'En Pleine Barbarie,' *L'Ordre*, November 11th 1938.
23 Albert Bayet, 'Une Telle Barbarie! . . . Le monde s'indigne! – La France se tait', in *La Lumière*, November 18th 1938.
24 *Le Populaire*, November 17th 1938.
25 *L'Epoque*, November 23rd 1938.
26 See *Le Populaire*, December 6th 1938.
27 Telegram from Rublee to Hull, no. 1334, November 19th 1938, FRUS 1938, I, pp. 883–4.
28 Note from Ribbentrop, RM 266, December 9th 1938, DGFP, Series D, IV, pp. 481–2. Telegrams from E. Phipps (British Ambassador to France) to Halifax, no. 404, December 7th 1938, and no. 407, December 8th 1938, DBRFP, Third Series, Vol. III, p. 389 and pp. 396–9.
29 Telegram from Wilson to Hull, no. 2117, December 15th 1938, FRUS 1938, I, pp. 871–3.
30 Memorandum from Messersmith, November 14th 1938, FRUS 1938, II, pp. 396–8.
31 Telegram from Hull to Wilson, no. 201, November 14th 1938, FRUS 1938, II, pp. 398–9.
32 Telegram from Dieckhoff to Ribbentrop, no. 329, November 14th 1938, DGFP, Series D, IV, pp. 639–40.
33 Telegram from Catt to Hull, November 11th 1938, Department of State Doc. no. 862.4016/1814.

34 Letter from U. J. Proeller, November 16th 1938, Department of State Doc. no. 862.4016.
35 Annexe dispatch no. 639 American Legation Tegucigalpa, Department of State Doc. 1993 GDG.
36 Welles Report, November 17th 1938, Department of State Doc. no. 840, 48/911 1/2.
37 See Arthur D. Morse, *While Six Million Died: A Chronicle of American Apathy* (New York and London, 1968), p. 251.
38 Department of State Doc. no. 862.4016/1841.
39 Doc. November 15th 1938, Department of State no. 840 48/900 1/2.
40 Letter. Franklin D. Roosevelt to Myron Taylor, November 23rd 1938, President's Secretary's File (Confidential File: State), Franklin D. Roosevelt Library, Hyde Park, N.Y.
41 *New York Times*, November 23rd 1938; dispatch of American Ambassador to Germany, November 23rd 1938, Department of State Doc. 862.4016/1893.
42 Arthur D. Morse, *op. cit.*, pp. 274–94.

EPILOGUE

1 Henry Torrès, *Accusés hors série* (Paris, 1957).
2 Basch was later shot, with his wife, by the Germans.
3 Testimony collected by Dr A. Cuenot at the end of the war, and preserved in his archives at Arcachon. The authors are particularly grateful to Dr Cuenot for having made his personal records of the Grynszpan case available to them.
4 Reichsministerium für Volksaufklärung und Propaganda, File no. 988 F 63, DZA, Potsdam.
5 *New York Times*, September 8th 1940.
6 *Goebbels Tagebücher* (Zurich, 1948), p. 81.
7 Helmut Heiber, 'Der Fall Grünspan', in *Vierteljahreshefte für Zeitgeschichte*, Heft 2, 1957.
8 Reichministerium für Volksaufklärung und Propaganda, File no. 979 F 71, DZA, Potsdam.
9 Collected by Emmanuel Feinermann on October 27th 1971 at Arcachon.
10 Letter from the Director of German Radio to the Minister of Propaganda, Berlin, March 23rd 1942. See files at the Centre de Documentation Juive Contemporaine, Paris.

11 *Goebbels Tagebücher* (Zurich, 1948), p. 152.
12 Evidence given by Schlegelberger at the trial of Diewerge, Court of Essen, January 18th 1966. See files at the Centre de Documentation Juive Contemporaine, Paris.
13 *L'Humanité*, November 8th 1938.

Selective Bibliography

ARCHIVES CONSULTED

GERMANY

Berlin: Geheimes Staatsarchiv, Berlin–Dahlem. Secret archives.
German Democratic Republic: Deutsches Zentralarchiv Potsdam.
   For the Grynszpan case.
German Federal Republic: Institut für Zeitgeschichte Munich;
   archives in various cities in the Republic relating to the period
   covered by this book.

UNITED STATES

National Archives, Washington.
Reports of American ambassadors and consuls in Germany during the
   period covered by this book.

FRANCE

Archives of Dr A. Cuenot, Arcachon. For the Grynszpan case.
Centre de Documentation Juive Contemporaine, Paris. French Police
   files on the Grynszpan case.

GREAT BRITAIN

Wiener Library, London. Collection of testimonies and reports by
   survivors of the 'Crystal Night'.

ISRAEL

Jewish Historical General Archives, Jerusalem. Yad Washem Institute, Jerusalem: files on the International Conference on the Refugees, Evian, 1938; testimonies by survivors of the 'Crystal Night'.

COLLECTIONS OF PUBLISHED DOCUMENTS

International Military Tribunal: Trial of the Major War Criminals. Proceedings and documents (Nuremberg, 1947 ff.).

Actes du Comité Intergouvernemental pour les réfugiés, Evian, du 6 au 15 juillet 1938 (Paris, 1938).

Documents of German Foreign Policy 1918–1945. From the Archives of the German Foreign Ministry. Series C, 1933–1937; Series D, 1937–1945 (London, HMSO, 1949 ff.; Washington, 1957–1966, 1949–1964).

Documents on British Foreign Policy 1919–1939: Second Series, London, HMSO, 1946–1965; Third Series, London, HMSO, 1949–1955.

Livre blanc sur les rapports germano – polonais (Paris, 1940).

GENERAL WORKS ON THE PERSECUTION OF THE JEWS BY THE THIRD REICH

Ball-Kaduri, Jakob, *Das Leben der Juden in Deutschland* (Frankfurt am Main, Europäische Verlagsanstalt 1963). The life of the Jews in Germany described by an Israeli historian.

Blau, Bruno, *Das Ausnahmerecht der Juden in Deutschland 1933–1945* 'Düsseldorf, 1954). Documents on anti-Jewish legislation in Germany.

Bramstead, Ernest, *Goebbels and National-Socialist Propaganda 1925–1945* (London, 1965).

Esh, Shaul, *Between Discrimination and Extermination*, Yad Washem Studies II (Jerusalem, 1958). The author was an Israeli historian who disappeared.

Friedman, Philipp, *Jewish Catastrophe and Heroism* (Jerusalem, 1960).

Genschel, Helmut, *Die Verdrängung der Juden aus der Wirtschaft im III Reich* (Göttingen, 1966). An excellent study of the plundering of Jewish property by the Nazis.

Grossmann, Kurt R., *Emigration* (Frankfurt am Main, Europäische Verlagsanstalt, 1969). A history of the emigration of the victims of Nazism by the former Secretary General of the German Section of the League of the Rights of Man.

Hilberg, Raul, *The Destruction of the European Jews* (Chicago, 1961).

Lamm, Hans, *Uber die innere und äussere Entwicklung des Deutschen Judentums im III. Reich* (Erlangen, 1951). A thesis on the history of the Jews in the Third Reich.

Levin, Nora, *The Holocaust: The Destruction of European Jewry 1933–1945* (New York, 1968).

Morse, Arthur D., *While Six Million Died: A Chronicle of American Apathy* (New York and London, 1968).

Poliakov, Léon, *Le Bréviaire de la Haine* (Paris, 1951).

Scharf, Andrew, *The British Press and Jews Under Nazi Rule 1933–1945* (London, 1964).

Scheffler, Wolfgang, *Juden Verfolgung im III. Reich, 1933–1945* (Berlin, 1960).

Shirer, William L., *The Rise and Fall of the Third Reich: A History of Nazi Germany* (New York, 1960).

Tenenbaum, Joseph L., *Race and Reich: The Story of an Epoch* (New York, 1956).

Vermeil, Edmond, 'Le Racisme Allemand,' *Cahiers Rationalistes*, 73 (January 1939). A speech given on November 12th 1938, introduced by Paul Langevin.

Wischnitzer, Mark, *To Dwell in Safety: The Story of Jewish Migration since 1800*, Philadelphia, 1948.

WORKS ON THE PERSECUTION OF THE JEWS IN SPECIFIC REGIONS OF GERMANY: A SHORT SELECTION

BADEN–WÜRTTEMBERG

Dokumente über die Verfolgung der Jüdischen Bürger in Baden–Württemberg, 1933–1945 (2 vols, Stuttgart, 1966 and 1968).

BERLIN

Andreas-Friedrich, Ruth, *A Berlin sous les Nazis* (Paris, 1966).

FRANKFURT AM MAIN

Dokumente zur Geschichte der Frankfurter Juden 1933–1945 (Frankfurt am Main, 1963).

MUNICH

Lamm, Hans, *Von Juden in München* (Munich, 1958–59).

WORKS ON THE GRYNSZPAN CASE

Diewerge, Wolfgang, *Anschlag gegen den Frieden* (Munich, 1939). The Yellow Book written by one of the Nazi participants in the case.

Dumoulin, Pierre, *Un Attentat contre la France* (Paris, 1942). 'Pierre Dumoulin' is a pseudonym; the book was written by Friedrich Grimm (see below), one of the Nazi participants in the case.

Ferdonnet, Paul, 'Toute la vérité sur l'affaire Grynszpan'. A document in the archives at Potsdam.

Grimm, Friedrich, *40 Jahre Dienst am Recht* (Bonn, 1953).

Heiber, Helmut, 'Der Fall Grünspan,' in *Vierteljahreshefte für Zeitgeschichte*, Heft 2 (1957), p. 136.

Kaul, Friedrich Karl, *Der Fall des Herschel Grynszpan* (East Berlin, 1965). A report based on the archives at Potsdam by an East German lawyer who has specialized in the study of war crimes.

Torrès, Henry, *Accusés hors série* (Paris, 1957).

PUBLICATIONS ON THE POGROM OF 1938

Bonte, Florimond, *Les Pogroms de la Croix gammée* (Paris, 1938). The author is a former Communist deputy.

Bruce, Michael, *Tramp Royal* (London, 1954). Memoirs of a former British diplomat sent to Berlin at the time of the pogrom.

Kochan, Lionel, *Pogrom – November 10, 1938* (London, 1957). The most precise existing study of the 'Crystal Night', by a historian who has worked on the archives of the Wiener Library, London.

Graml, Hermann, 'Der 9. November 1938', a pamphlet of the Bundeszentrale für Heimatdienst (Bonn, 1955), no. 2.

Mann, Heinrich, *Der Pogrom* (Zurich, 1939). A book written by a German writer in exile.

'The Pogroms in Germany', Parliamentary Debates, House of

Commons, Official Report, Vol. 341, no. 10, November 21st 1938. The debate in the House of Commons, London, on the 'Crystal Night'.

Weizmann, Chaim, *Trial and Error: The Autobiography of Chaim Weizmann* (New York, 1949). A report by the first president of Israel, in London at the time of the pogrom.

'Ein Waffenstillstandstag' (Doc. BDIC., Paris). A clandestine pamphlet in German on the pogroms of November 1938 and world opinion, circulated with covers boasting the merits of a shampoo from the Lloyd perfumery.

NEWSPAPERS

The principal articles concerning this subject are listed in the 'Notes to the Text'.

Index